# EASY MURDER

# EASY MURDER

## Based on a True Story

by
## Zale Flannery

ISBN-13: 978-1724654649
ISBN-10: 1724654640

*To Andy and Dorothy for their great memories and to Kevin who was there every step of the way*

# March 11, 1958 – EVELYN

E velyn Smith sat in the car, tapping her fingernail against
the steering wheel. She was angry she had to wait for him,
but really, that was hardly different than the usual way Danny
Russo treated her. He liked to meet on these dirt rutted roads
in small towns along the highway. This one, Valley Falls Road,
was in Vernon, Connecticut, where nothing ever happened.
They had used it before, because you could hardly see it from
the larger paved road running by and very few people ever
drove down it. There were woods on each side of the road
with no houses. The place looked utterly bleak, with no leaves
on the tall, sad trees and nothing but mud on the side of
the road. She had no idea why the road was there, except
for someone to get into the fields beyond. It certainly was
deserted, like at least a half dozen other roads Danny had
directed her to meet him over the past 4 years. She fished
around her handbag for a cigarette. She needed one. She
had grown to hate these clandestine meetings. She shook
her head in disbelief over how much she had enjoyed them
when they started. Sneaking around to be sure no one saw
them, taking opposite routes to the same spot and getting
excited when his car met hers, in whatever rutted, back road
they found. Sometimes she wished she could feel that antici-
pation and giddiness again. It was a great feeling coming from

her staid marriage and her boring home. But, that was over now. Now Evelyn wanted this to be all over and she wanted her money back.

Evelyn lit the cigarette and thought back on her first happy days with Danny. Yes, Danny Russo was an important Vice President for the Penn Manufacturing Company and yes, he was handsome, funny and beautifully dressed. No wonder she was impressed, she was a new secretary still in her 20s and excited that she had been offered such an important job. In the beginning she just wanted to make a good impression. And, she was good at what she did: typed like a demon, took shorthand as fast as anyone could talk, and she knew she was not bad looking. In fact, she thought being pretty was part of the appeal. After all, Danny was a forty two year old handsome young man. To Evelyn it seemed she had reached a pinnacle with a good job and a good salary. She was proud of what she had accomplished.

Five years ago, when she first signed up to take the secretarial class at the local junior college, everyone, her husband, her parents, even her friends, were skeptical. They didn't know why she wanted to work and they certainly didn't want to know why she should think of anything but having a family and taking care of her children and her husband. It became clear to Evelyn that unless she did something on her own her life would consist of cleaning, cooking and waiting endlessly for her husband to come home from work. In almost 6 years of marriage, she never got pregnant and she suspected her husband blamed her in some way for that shortcoming. It became clear that life would consist of daily boring chores and an endless conversation with her husband on how they could save more money for their old age. At first Evelyn thought her husband would like her interest in working. If nothing else, it would mean more money which would mean more savings. But it didn't work out that way. Yes, her husband liked to put a larger deposit into their bank account each week, and he duly pecked her on the cheek as a thank you when she handed over the cash, but when she suggested they use some of the money for fun like dinners out, seeing a movie or going to a dance with friends, he refused. Evelyn quickly figured out that it would be best not to tell her husband exactly what she got in her paycheck each week. The money she contributed to their old age fund represented only part of the money Evelyn earned. Each week when she got her pay envelope and each time she got a raise she kept some of the cash to herself. This gave her some money to buy nice clothes and to get her hair done. She'd show the new outfits to her husband and then give him an absurdly low amount that they cost. He was clueless, and never realized that she was spending much more than she said shopping and dressing for the office. When she considered how much she hadn't told her husband over the 4 years she had been at Penn Manufacturing she realized it wasn't so surprising that he had no clue about her relationship with Danny.

The Penn Manufacturing Company was very well respected in central Connecticut and Evelyn was proud to say she worked there. By the end of her first week she also learned a great deal about how Danny Russo got to be the youngest Vice President in the company's history. As the other secretaries were quick to tell her, Danny worked at the company for about 10 years. He came from a small tool and dye factory that Penn Manufacturing purchased. He was a mechanical engineer, which was actually more of a practical engineer, since he hadn't been to engineering school. That wasn't very unusual in the late 1940s. Boys with engineering aptitude were often trained on the job to do basic engineering work on machine parts. Danny arrived with a good recommendation from his former employer and was put to work in the basic machine group working on the engines for Penn Manufacturing's largest client, Sikorsky Helicopters.

The aerospace industry in Connecticut had been booming since the beginning of the war. All through the 1940s and 1950s, having a job with any of the companies that supplied parts or built airplanes and helicopters for the government was a golden opportunity. For Danny it carried more than the benefit of steady work and a good income. Being involved in aerospace production he was able to leap ahead in his field which was practical engineering and manufacturing. When the war started, Danny's former small tool and dye company was one of the suppliers to Pratt & Whitney, located in East Hartford, Connecticut. Pratt and Whitey was the major engine manufacturer for military aircraft for the US Government. Everyone who worked in Danny's small factory was immediately exempt from military service. Danny knew a few guys who tried to sign up for the army and were turned down because they worked at an aerospace supplier company. He even knew a few guys who lied about where they worked so they could get into the Army. Danny thought that was the stupidest idea he had ever heard. Who would want to go to get killed when they had a legitimate reason to stay home? Danny thought they were stupid, which was his answer to anyone who did something he didn't or wouldn't do.

When he arrived at Penn Manufacturing, the story was that Danny came up with a very good idea on a small change in an engine structure that would make the engine for a helicopter run more efficiently. He approached his supervisor about the change but was told to do his work and not get involved in areas he knew nothing about. Danny surmised that the supervisor did not understand what he was suggesting, so he went over his supervisor's head, taking his idea to the manager of the department. The manager liked the idea a great deal. The manager knew siding with Danny would bring some discord to the engineering group, but this idea was very good. He took it forward. No one was surprised that Danny's supervisor was livid, but everyone was surprised that the manager agreed it was a great idea and took it to the higher ups. It turned out everyone involved with the manufacturing project thought it was a very good idea, indeed, and Sikorsky, the client, who as one of Penn Manufacturing's largest clients was treated very carefully, was called in to discuss the change. The idea was tested and accepted. From that moment on, Danny's star was rising, although his supervisor would never forgive him. Danny's attitude about his supervisor was his typical reaction to anyone who wasn't as quick, smart or forceful as he was: too bad. Danny couldn't be bothered with the stupid people who didn't get how smart he was. He called anyone who couldn't agree with him "stupid idiots." It might have been true much of the time, but it wasn't true all the time, which meant Danny left enemies in his wake where ever he went.

The success of his first suggestion made Danny fearless. He began to question much of the structure of the work that the engineers in the machining group were doing, and some of his ideas were quite good. His promotions were coming very fast and Senior management at the firm began to think they had a boy wonder in their midst, giving Danny more and more leeway to review the work being done. Promotions followed quickly. Danny responded by becoming pushy and a showoff. With his frequent bonuses he bought a new wardrobe and car, he talked about all the women he dated, which was not very well received since he was married. But most of all he talked about how smart he was and how dumb so many of the people at the company were.

Danny's hunger for attention and the money the promotions were producing made him desperate to keep the suggestions coming. He stayed late at night to rifle through others' desks hoping to steal ideas he could claim were his. He sought out three or four of the younger engineers, especially Ed Quinn, Jeff Lester and Mark Mazzo, who he thought showed promise. He made friends with them by taking them to ballgames and prize fights. He called the outings the "guys nights". He was the only one of the "guys nights" group who was married, so the younger engineers didn't question why Danny wasn't going home to his wife like the older engineers in the company. Besides, the three single guys in the "guys nights" were having too much fun. And Danny always picked up the tab.

During these outings Danny plied the guys with beers and talked about their projects at the company. Pretty soon the younger men were sharing their work and more importantly, their ideas with him. Danny always told them how smart they were to work so hard. He also gently told them that most of their ideas had already been vetted with the higher ups. Of course they hadn't, but Danny knew he could pass off the better ideas he heard as his own at the company and get the credit for any that worked. He hoped the younger men didn't catch on too quickly with his game of stealing their ideas, but whatever they did, Danny figured some booze and/or cash would make them keep silent.

Danny seldom made bad suggestions to senior management, but when he did he quickly covered it up by saying the idea came from one of the other engineers. This happened one day when Ed Quinn, a "guy's night" regular, heard that Danny was telling senior management a recent failed engine trial was based on Ed's work. The idea had been Danny's and Ed was furious. Danny realized it immediately and asked Ed to meet him in the john. Danny stood in front of the mirror, next to Ed who was red faced and leering at him. Danny had never seen Ed so angry. Danny put on his most sincere, caring face and tried to get Ed to calm down

"Look Ed, I am really sorry. I thought that change to the engine casing was going to be a great idea. And if it had worked like I planned, I wanted to include you so the company would let me work with you on its development. I never thought it would fail, and I was hoping with your work and my ideas we could make it really big."

Ed looked at Danny in the mirror dubiously. He was not falling for this line of bullshit.

"Really? Then why didn't you tell me about it before you submitted the prototype so I could look it over and see if it was going to work? You're not the only engineer at Penn who can follow a blueprint."

Danny turned Ed towards him placing his hands on Ed's shoulders. He looked Ed in the eye.

"I was going to tell you about it on our "guy's night" last week, but you had to cancel and I never had a chance. I didn't want to miss the opportunity to keep you in the mix so when the conversation came up with the higher ups the next day I told them you were working on it too. I never intended for you to take any blame for it not working, I thought it would be the beginning of us being partners in lots of new developments."

Ed was torn. Yes, he had been out with Danny on the "guy's nights" more than once but he still didn't buy the entire story. He stood staring Danny in the eye. Danny realized he had not won Ed over. He slowly pulled a roll of $20 bills out of his pocket and stuffed them into Ed's shirt pocket. It was clear the money was to keep Ed quiet. Ed stepped back from Danny's grip, turned and walked out of the john.

Ed took Danny's cash but let everyone around them know Danny's game. Ed even told people that Danny had "bought him off." Danny might be smart, but the scuttle about him was that he was devious and selfish. Danny's mode of operation was that all the good ideas were his and all the bad ideas were from other guys. Like most businesses, the lower level people knew lots more than the senior people about how everyone behaved. It took awhile but by the time Senior management got wise to him, Danny had reached the title of Vice President. The CEO was willing to put up with Danny's failings, hoping to save Danny's good ideas and ignore the anger he caused. But more and more people were seeing Danny for what he was and the atmosphere around him was becoming toxic.

The first few months Evelyn worked with Danny were normal, except that she too found out things about Danny that went beyond typing memos and taking shorthand. She knew he had a wimpy wife who he paid very little attention to. In fact, most of the time the wife called, Evelyn was told to say Danny was in a meeting. Evelyn tried not to mention her own husband around Danny. She thought it would make Danny like her less, and she did want him to like her. She knew Danny gambled a lot. He loved the horses, fights and cards. She could tell when he won because he would be in a good mood, laughing when she arrived in the morning and telling her he wished he could bring her flowers but didn't want to make the other girls jealous. When he lost he tried to shrug it off, but a couple of times she could tell that he was angry or worried. She heard him on the phone talking about bets he was placing and bets he owed. Not all of the calls were pleasant. A few times she heard him pleading for time to make payments, but after he hung up the phone he always put on a happy face and smiled at her. She wasn't sure if the gambling made him money in the long run or cost him money, but he always had a new car and dressed beautifully. He couldn't be losing that much.

Danny also had a very bad temper. His anger was directed at anyone who, in his words, was "an imbecile" and "stupid", but he was also very rough on anyone who called him out for a mistake or crossing the line on the truth. Unfortunately, Danny was most volatile if the person was Jewish. He often said he hated "those dirty Jews". Evelyn learned to steer clear of any references to people Danny lashed out about. It scared her to see him become red faced while he relived every fight with anyone who tangled with him. He was always ready to fight. Anything could set him off and he would start acting crazy, screaming, swearing, and pounding his hand on the desk, chair or wall. She was scarred when she saw how angry he could be. One day she walked into his office, closed the door and began to go over the calls she answered while Danny was in a meeting. She mentioned a Mr. Kaufman who was asking her to set up a meeting with Danny. Suddenly Danny slammed the desk with his hand and screamed,

"Don't ever make an appointment with that dirty Kike. I have no use for him. He is so stupid. He questioned my suggestion on the recent redesign of the housing for the motor. He is out to get me, but I'm going to get him first. He's going to regret those lies he pushed. He's an asshole."

It took about five minutes for Danny to calm down and for Evelyn to feel she could open Danny's office door. She was sure the whole office had heard the screaming, she only hoped they didn't know who Danny was screaming about. She thought Mr. Kaufman was a real gentleman. He had a quiet voice and always spoke to her politely on the phone. It was impossible to imagine him erupting like Danny over something like a question on the housing for a motor. She was going to have to make up some story to avoid giving him a date and time to meet with Danny. Evelyn shook her head realizing that there were parts of working with Danny at Penn that were less than enjoyable.

Evelyn discovered that besides the few Jews who worked there, Danny had other enemies at Penn Manufacturing. More than one higher up had approached her to see what Danny was up to, and there were calls from the CEO for Danny to appear to discuss "issues" from time to time. In fact, Danny's issues with the CEO and other Vice Presidents ended badly. After one particularly contentious meeting, Danny returned to his office and announced he was becoming a consultant to the company. He'd keep his office when he was working on a project, but he wouldn't be a fulltime employee anymore. He was going to move to New Jersey with his wife and commute back to Connecticut when he was needed. He tried to put a good face on it saying he had great opportunities in New Jersey. Evelyn thought differently.

But that was after Evelyn and Danny had become much more than just a handsome Vice President and his pretty young secretary.

Evelyn took another drag on the cigarette. Where was he? She was glad she had stopped at the little convenience store right off the highway. It gave her a chance to pick up some groceries, which would help with any suspicions her husband might have when she got home. She also bought the cigarettes. She liked the way the two men in the store admired her outfit. She always dressed up because it made her seem older and in control. Today she had on her new brown coat with a matching brown sweater, a brown and beige plaid skirt and a pair of brown lizard skin pumps. She thought the outfit was perfect, and the men in the store and the gas station attendant all seemed to think it was pretty sweet. One of them even whistled.

Evelyn tried to remember what she was wearing the first time Danny asked her to work late. She knew he was dressed, as always, in a beautiful suit, starched shirt and silk tie. He always wore shined shoes. She was fascinated by his looks. At about 6 feet 2 inches tall, with dark, thick hair and a gorgeous smile, he looked like a movie star. He must have weighed about 200 pounds because he was quite large, but all of it was in the right place. A big part of the secretarial gossip was what Danny looked like under the shirt and suit. It was hard to ignore. Her husband, she had to admit, didn't quite measure up. He was about 5 feet 9 inches tall and weighed about 155 pounds with brown hair and brown eyes. He was fine, but not in Danny's league. Evelyn smiled, she just remembered that the first night she and Danny worked late together she had on her favorite red dress. It hugged her body in a very nice way, emphasizing her rounded breasts, flat stomach and nice butt. Danny had mentioned how attractive she looked the first time she wore the dress with its matching red and white scarf and beautiful black pumps. After his first comment, Evelyn made the dress a bi-weekly pick in her wardrobe selection. She knew when she looked good and hoped he appreciated her efforts.

That first night of working late surprised Evelyn. Danny had a big presentation the next day and asked her to stay to help get it finalized. She called her husband and told him she would be late. After everyone left, Danny and Evelyn sat at his desk and worked through the information. She watched him write his notes and lean back in his chair to think, as he said, of the best angle to persuade the executives he was on the right path for a change he was suggesting. At one point he got up and got them both coffee. It was such a reversal to have him serving her she was amazed that he thought of it. She couldn't believe he was listening to her suggestions and thinking about using some of the language she was offering.

He made her feel very important. It was all very professional. When they finished he thanked her for her time and offered to walk her to her car. He held the car door open for her to get in and thanked her again for her help. She blushed when he said she was one of the smartest people he knew at Penn Manufacturing. She looked at him in the rearview mirror as she drove away. She loved every minute of being with him. She went to bed that night dreaming of his thick dark hair and large strong hands.

About a week later Danny asked her to stay late again. She eagerly agreed and called her husband to say she had to stay. Evelyn hoped that this evening would be as interesting and exciting as the week before. She had no idea how exciting it was going to become. This time when everyone left Danny opened a drawer and pulled out a bottle of whiskey with two glasses. He made a joke about drinking too much coffee in one day and would she like to have a drink? When she said, "Yes", he held up a glass for her to take and poured about an inch of liquor into it. Her hand shook a bit as she took a sip. She looked around the office to see what work needed to be done, but there was not a paper on his desk. Danny was standing very close to her.

Evelyn looked up into his beautiful brown eyes rimmed with thick dark lashes and asked if she could do anything for him. Danny just smiled and waited. Time stood still. Then she reached up and pulled his head toward her and met his lips. It was a very soft, sweet kiss. He pulled away and smiled again, never taking his eyes from her. He moved his hand to hers to take her glass. He set it down slowly onto his desk. Suddenly he pulled her to him molding his body against hers.

He began to devour her mouth with hot, wet kisses. She had never felt such a sensation before. He was so strong he could have broken her in half, but she loved the feeling of power-lessness. He kissed her neck, her face, her hair, all the while pulling her closer to him. She could feel him through her dress and she had to decide what to do. But, there wasn't anything she could do. He was in charge. Suddenly he put his hand under her dress, moved up her leg and began to mas-sage her crotch. She went wild. It was unreal, in the office, to feel like this.

And then he stopped. He let her go and gave her a min-ute to catch her breath. He slowly handed her back her drink all the while smiling at her. She took a few sips and stead-ied herself. Danny asked her if she would like to work late again some time. He watched to see what her reaction would be. She took a deep breath and whispered, "Yes". He smiled again and said,

"I'll walk you to your car. And next time I'll tell you where we can meet, because this office is not the place for you and me to be together"

Evelyn understood completely.

One week later, the first time they met in a motel was like magic. Danny was there before her and brought some wine and flowers. The flowers smelled wonderful. Watching him un-dress was mesmerizing. His beautiful shirt and tie came off quickly. He wore one of those skinny, tight fitting undershirts with no sleeves. She had only seen them in advertisements because her husband wore plain, boxy white undershirts with short sleeves. Danny's shoulders and arms bulged with mus-cles and she was transfixed as he undid his belt and zipper.

As he pulled off his pants and socks he turned to her and said,

"Your turn now. I love undressing beautiful women."

And he did. Piece by piece he peeled off her clothing. Then he lifted her up and laid her on the bed. He kissed her and licked her and touched her until she was helpless. He kneaded and sucked her breasts and nipples. Then he rolled on top of her and entered her. It was heavenly. He was heavy and warm and everywhere. She could not get her breath but didn't want him to move. Except then he began to move and it was even better. They made love like she had never made love before. He stopped and moved down her body, kissing her as he made his way over her breasts to her stomach and then to her mound. He spread her wide and licked and sucked at her until she screamed, then he moved back up and into her again. This went on for a long time. She was limp and liquid and happy. Except she realized she could never tell anyone she knew just how happy she was right at that moment. She closed her eyes and decided to enjoy all the sensations pulsing through her. It didn't matter that she couldn't share this with anyone else. She was excited to be experiencing it herself. She would remember how this felt forever.

And here she was, 4 years later, waiting for Danny again. There had been lots of waits over the 4 years. He was a busy guy with his work, his "guys nights out" and his wife. He had to fit her in whenever he could and sadly, she had settled for that arrangement. When they were together Evelyn felt it was all worthwhile. He still made her feel like no one else, least of all her husband, had ever made her feel. She had learned to put up with the yearning she had for Danny and she had learned to be available whenever his schedule allowed. He had an endless string of motels, hidden roads and out of the way lunch counters where they would meet. His favorite motels where ones that she could park her car in front of the room and he could park on the other side of the building so their cars were never together. He thought of everything, like leaving the key to a hotel room in the top drawer of her desk so she could find it with its fob telling her the motel name and address. She thought he was very clever about how to hide their meetings, but then she thought that he was so clever it was like he had done it all before. He was practiced at it. And that made her pause. At one point she thought it would end when he moved with his mousey wife to a town in New Jersey called Montclair, but it didn't. He was back in Connecticut almost every week. But she knew exactly when their meetings changed. It was six months ago.

Evelyn remembered that night six months ago. After making love Danny talked with her about some great investments he had. His stocks were bringing in huge amounts of money and he was loving the freedom it gave him. He told her he was making a great return every month and if she was interested he might be able to get her some of the action. Evelyn knew almost nothing about investments, but she did like money and wished she had more than her salary and her husband's paycheck. She asked,

"Danny, if I gave you some money could I get it back quickly so my husband wouldn't notice the money is gone?"

Evelyn wasn't sure how an investment through Danny would work and she was worried her husband might find out if she took the money out of their account without discussing it with him. Danny seemed to be thinking about how it would be structured. He looked back at her seriously,

"I'm not sure how much you are interested in investing, but if you put a few thousand dollars into the investment I am sure that wouldn't be a problem. In fact, if it continues to pay the way it has been throwing cash I would say you'd have your original investment back before your husband would even know it was gone. Then all the additional income and your original amount could be yours without worrying about your husband at all."

Evelyn was sold. She agreed to give Danny $4,000 but told him she would need it back in two months. It was now four months later and she hadn't seen any cash. She was desperate to put the money back in the account before her husband found out it was gone. Just the weekend before Evelyn had to hide the bank statements her husband asked to see. She told him she took the savings and checking account information to the office to balance the checkbook in her spare time at work. She said she left the statements in her desk. Her husband seemed to buy the lie, but Evelyn knew it couldn't last long. She had to get the money back into the account immediately.

In the last two months, Evelyn had done everything she could to get Danny to return her money. She telephoned Danny incessantly, she threatened to go to his wife and tell her everything. She swore she would never be with him again if he didn't pay her back immediately. She even wrote him a letter pleading for the money back. She was terrified her husband would find out she took the money and that she and Danny were so involved. She never sent the letter because she couldn't be sure Danny's wife wouldn't open it. She stuck it into the bottom drawer of her desk at work with Danny's name on the sealed envelope. She thought she might give it to him the next time he came to the office, whenever that would be. She was running out of ideas of how to make Danny pay her back. Every time they met Danny had an excuse why he couldn't give her the money when he appeared. But when they set up this meeting in Vernon, Evelyn told Danny he had to bring the money. She insisted this time was the last time she would be put off. She was going to do something to get the $4,000 back. He agreed to meet her in Vernon on this abandoned road to get it straightened out.

What Danny didn't know was that she was ready for him. Evelyn spent hours thinking of what she could do to make Danny give her the money. She knew he was afraid of being caught in an affair, but so was she. Exposing their relationship was not a solution. She could confront Danny's wife with what had been going on but could not imagine the wife giving her the money she needed. In the end she had to find a way to scare Danny into giving her the money. He was so much bigger and stronger than she was that her only hope was if she used a gun to threaten him. She was convinced that only the thought of her hurting him would make Danny fork over the cash. She had taken her husband's handgun from his closet and loaded it with bullets. She had never shot a gun before, but she was desperate and thought this was the only way to make Danny see she would not be put off again. She had the gun in a small paper bag on the car seat next to her. If Danny became difficult she planned to pull it out of the bag and point it at him to make him pay her. She hoped that just seeing the gun would make Danny realize how desperate she was.

She threw the cigarette butt out the window and lit another one. She looked in the rearview mirror and saw Danny drive up in his new Cadillac. He left his car on the dirt road behind hers. She took a deep breath and hoped she had the nerve to go through with this. But mostly she hoped Danny had the money. It would be so easy to take it from him and leave. Watching him walk to the car in his beautiful overcoat, soft leather gloves and hat, she saw again how handsome he was and she knew she would miss how he made love to her. But it had to end and this looked like the end. There was a bittersweet feeling knowing that it was over but Evelyn couldn't fool herself forever. Danny had a wife and she had a husband. Danny had never suggested to her that they had a future together. He never even said she was his preferred woman. She didn't even want to think about him in other relationships with women who were not his wife. How did she know she was the only one? He could be seeing multiple women. It angered her. Yes, this was the end, and sadly, if she had never given him her money it could have ended with a sweet goodbye. But it was not to be. She could rack it up to how young and impressionable she had been in the beginning. The sex had been great but unfortunately, she needed to replace the money so there was no sweetness or fond memories to be had. This was business and he owed her the cash.

Danny walked to the passenger side of her car and opened the door. He looked beautiful, as usual. He leaned in and asked how she was. Evelyn said she was fine and asked why he left his car behind hers on the dirt road. He shrugged and said there were more tire marks on the unpaved road behind her. Evelyn wasn't sure what that meant, but he was so careful about everything she ignored it.

"Get in."

He sat on the seat, leaning against the door looking at her. He was not going to make this easy. She pulled on her cigarette, hoping he would say something or do something. The silence was horrible. He looked out the window at the woods and the grey sky. He did not look happy, but then, neither was she. Evelyn couldn't bear the silence.

"I hope you brought the money."

He stared at her. There was not one shred of caring in his look. He seemed annoyed. She suddenly realized there was no way she would ever see the money again. In total despair she leaned her forehead against the driver's wheel and closed her eyes. She could hear him breathing. She turned her head towards him and saw from the corner of her eye that he had picked up the bag with the gun. She heard a rustle and suddenly looked up. He was holding her husband's pistol in his gloved hand. She screamed and he shot twice.

# March 11, 1958 – DANNY

D anny got out of Evelyn's car slowly. Luckily no blood had splattered his coat. He still had the gun in his hand but thought it would be better to keep it than to leave it. He looked at Evelyn's body slumped over the steering wheel. His hands were shaking. He couldn't believe he pulled the trigger. In fact, he thought he pulled the trigger twice, but there was only one hole in Evelyn's head. He shut his eyes and tried to imagine what would happen next. He realized he had to act quickly because someone might have heard the shots. He couldn't stick around here because anyone could come down the road and he would be doomed. His Cadillac was not exactly a nondescript car. He willed his hands to stop shaking and tried to take some deep breaths so he could think more clearly. He looked again at the sky and hoped for rain, which would hide any tire marks from his car on the unpaved road. He got in his Cadillac, threw the gun and the paper bag on the seat next to him and backed down the road until he reached the paved street. No cars were coming so he pulled out and went in the opposite direction from the one he had come. He couldn't imagine why Evelyn had brought a loaded gun to their meeting and left it on the seat. He mumbled to himself,

"Talk about making it easy. I guess she wasn't as smart

as she thought. Where did she get a loaded gun, and why did she leave it on the seat? What a dumb bitch."

When Danny left to meet Evelyn earlier that afternoon he thought about how he could appease her. He didn't have the money she wanted. In fact, he had no idea when he might have the money she wanted. When he first took the cash from her he had promised Evelyn a great return on her investment and told her she could get her initial $4,000 back quickly. Well, that arrangement never worked out because the investment Danny talked her into was bogus. It never happened.

Danny thought that he might have to silence Evelyn because he couldn't pay her back. He wasn't sure how or what he would do to her, but he knew that he had to do something because his constant putting her off had come to an end. Her last call to him had been frantic and he knew she was desperate. He had never physically hurt Evelyn, but he thought he could strangle her easily. She was a small girl and didn't weigh half of what he did. The problem with that option was that he would have to dispose of her body. Then he wondered if he could scare her with some threat which would keep her quiet. The trouble was that Evelyn was already dealing with the threat of exposure because the money was gone and their relationship would be public as soon as the money scheme came to light. Danny couldn't think of a worse threat he could make, unless he threatened to kill her. He had no interest in seeing her again or continuing their relationship so maybe threatening her life was the way to go. That might make her calm down and he could try to find some cash in the next few months to pay her back.

Then as they sat in the car together and he opened the bag and saw the gun it just seemed so easy. It was a way to get away from this entire problem quickly. He probably shouldn't have jumped on it so fast, but it was a relief to have a solution before him. And, for better or worse now, he took the gun into his hand and solved his problem. With two quick shots he gained freedom from both her threats and his debts.

As he drove south towards New Jersey he thought of what he should do next. He would head back to Montclair which might mean no one would know he had been in Connecticut. He would have to dispose of the gun. Perhaps he could throw it in the river when he crossed the bridge near Hartford. Better yet, he would dismantle the gun so it couldn't be easily found. Then he would throw it in the river. He just had to be sure that no one was on the banks of the river when he threw it in. As long as no one saw him drop the gun in the water there was a good chance the murder weapon wouldn't be found. He had a vague idea that it would be harder to pin a murder on someone if the cops never found the weapon. There was a small pull off just over the bridge that people used to park their cars and walk back on the bridge sidewalk to see the skyline of Hartford ahead. He would stop there on his way south. The more he began to make plans the calmer he became. He kept thinking this would work out, but he had to figure out exactly what he would do and what he would say if anyone asked about Evelyn or this afternoon. He had to work at keeping calm. He knew that panicking would be the worst thing he could do. He kept telling himself, "Think, think....what would be best."

He began to format a plan in his head. It was easier to

think about what had to be done than what he had just done. He had to focus on the future, not on what just happened.

Tomorrow he would tell Penn Manufacturing that he was too busy in New Jersey at his new consulting jobs with the candy manufacturer, Cutter & Sons, and Harley Davidson to do any work in Connecticut. He didn't need the excuse to go to Hartford anymore to keep Evelyn quiet. It seemed very strange, but his problem with Evelyn was solved. He no longer owed her the money and he no longer had to worry about her exposing their relationship. His new consulting set ups in New Jersey had been good about giving him time to return to consult with Penn Manufacturing, but he'd tell the New Jersey people the project he was working on in Connecticut was winding down and he didn't need the time off any more. He would suggest to Penn Manufacturing that they give his office to someone else and recommend his secretary, Evelyn, to anyone who needed help. She was very good at her job.

The more he planned, the less his hands shook and his breathing leveled. Danny thought this just might work out.

Four hours later, after stopping on the Charter Oak Bridge and carefully dropping the dismantled gun over the guardrail when he was sure no one was looking from the shore, Danny was driving up to his home in Montclair, NJ. The trash bin had been pulled to the curb for the pickup the next day and Danny threw the paper bag that Evelyn had carried the gun in into the bin. He walked slowly into the house and heard his wife, Dee, in the kitchen making dinner. He thought he did a good job of small talking his way through dinner. He told Dee he was very tired from the long day and wanted to go to bed early. She was surprised since he usually stayed up late and watched old movies or the fights, but it was fine with her. He said good night and went to their bedroom.

The next morning, Danny called Penn Manufacturing and spoke to the CEO. He explained he was very busy at his new jobs and couldn't keep coming back to Connecticut. The CEO seemed uninterested, which made Danny think it was a good time to sever these ties. The two men were pleasant to each other and the conversation ended quickly.

To Danny's mind, everything was working out just fine.

One day later a local Vernon resident reported that a car had been parked on Valley Falls Road for a few days. It had not moved. Local police investigated and found a dead woman, slumped over the steering wheel with her head covered in blood. She appeared to be young and was well dressed. There was a bag of groceries in the back seat and a cigarette had burned out on her coat. Her purse in the car carried identification that she was Evelyn Smith of Norwich, Connecticut. Her car was registered to her husband. No suspect had been identified.

Police interviewed the cashier in the grocery store where Evelyn had purchased the food and the cigarettes. The cashier described her perfectly. The guy at the gas station also remembered seeing her. Neither of them remembered anyone else being in her car or with her. No one in the area could testify they saw any other car on the deserted road the day of Evelyn's murder. The police were at a standstill.

Danny read the newspaper report of the shooting in Connecticut the next morning. Dee, his wife, did not read the paper daily, but she might pick it up so he took the paper with him to the office and threw it into the trash in the men's room. Men were always coming into the john and leaving behind newspapers. No one would notice anything strange that it was there.

Danny went to his desk at Cutter and Sons and worked straight through the day.

# TWELVE YEARS EARLIER
## September 1, 1946 – MARIA

Maria Russo sat slumped in the chair in the corner of her kitchen. She and Vito had done all they could to raise the boys well, but they continually got into trouble. Their two daughters had married and were well settled, but her three sons were a constant trial. She knew Frank, the oldest, was slow witted and Tommy, the youngest, was too arrogant and belligerent for his own good, especially when he drank. But her Danny, the beautiful middle son, the one that was smart and successful was up to no good and she knew it.

Danny was her only married son. The marriage was not one Maria would have chosen, but it happened and that was the end of any other outcomes she could envision. They were Catholic. You married for life. Maria hoped Danny and his small family could be happy and successful, but Danny was not acting like a happy, successful husband should behave. Maria was distraught. She knew Danny thought she didn't see how he neglected his wife and his child. Danny thought Maria didn't know that he disappeared for days at a time and then acted as if he had been around every night. He thought she was stupid. In fact, he thought everyone was stupid but him. Maria worried Danny's endless weaving of the truth and hiding his actions would be his downfall. And it made her very angry. She couldn't understand why Danny didn't accept that he now had a wife and child who depended on him for more than just the rent money and groceries. Danny's wife, Nora, was a little dim, Maria could see that annoyed Danny, but the baby, Henry was an angel. Maria couldn't understand why Danny didn't appreciate the young life he had brought into this world and enjoy being with Henry every day. And Nora could have children, why not enjoy having more children and seeing them grow up. It was beyond Maria's comprehension.

Maria's sister, Appolina, spoke to her many times about Danny's attitude. From the time Danny was a teenager, Appolina told Maria Danny was too "big for his britches", as the saying went. He would come to no good if he didn't control himself. He felt he was bigger, better and smarter than everyone, and he did a poor job of hiding it from those who he should pay some respect. Appolina thought Danny lived as if he could get away with anything. At the time, Maria brushed Appolina off. Danny was just a strong personality. He would grow up and be a successful man. She was sure. Her other boys were not exceptional but Danny could be, if only he tried. Now it looked like Appolina was right. Maria couldn't think of a way to make Danny understand how much he could lose by his lies and indifference. If only she could make him understand that she had seen this before. A long time before.

Maria thought back to the days when she was a young woman in northern Italy. She remembered the moments when she was so angry she thought she would burst. But in Italy she took action and made things better. There was no action to take in this situation. Danny was doing everything he wanted. He wasn't listening to his mother. It was like Maria and her opinion no longer mattered to Danny. Maria felt helpless to change the situation. That is what made this so hard to bear. Maria was used to making things happen the way she thought they should happen. For so many years she told her husband and children what to do and they did it. She was not used to being handed a situation she had no control over with no option or opportunity for her to make it right. For 34 years in America she had controlled the outcome of her life. She married who she thought would be the easiest and most reliable man, she brow beat, or outright beat, her children to make them behave, and made pronouncements that could not be overruled. She was expert at getting her way or changing something to go her way. But Danny, married in his 20s and doing as he pleased with his family was different.... This she could not change.

Maria thought back to Italy. She lived in a noisy and rough family of two daughters and four brothers. Maria was the older girl, but her sister, Appolina, was only 11 months younger. The sisters looked very different. Maria was smart, tough, dour and plain. Appolina was lithe, happy and very pretty. But for all of the differences in looks, the sisters thought alike. Appolina ceded tactical control to Maria who she acknowledged was smarter, but Maria knew that Appolina was quick and fearless. Together they formed a strong alliance, which they needed in a family where everything was decided by the men.

The brothers were all older. Maria's father worked in the local marble quarry, and her brothers joined him there as soon as they were old enough. Maria's mother, Appolina and

Maria were responsible for the cooking, cleaning and sewing for all eight family members. As far as their father and brothers were concerned the women in the house were there to cater to their every need. In effect, Maria, her mother and Appolina were slaves to whatever the men wanted.

Maria's father was the king, and no one crossed him. He could be harsh and vindictive. He was not well liked in the town and didn't seem to care what people thought about him. He worked hard at the quarry and thought that when he came home he should be in absolute control. Everything in the house and the family was done according to his wishes. Maria felt no sense of warmth towards her father. Other than doing his bidding, she wasn't sure he knew she was alive. Maria didn't know if or when she would get married, but it would never be to a cold, brutal man like her father.

Next came the brothers, and no one crossed them either. The boys were very cruel to the girls and at times, their mother. They made them do extra work for the fun of it, throwing food around the kitchen or tearing apart the beds so the girls would have to clean their mess. They often came home late for meals and insisted they be waited upon, even if the girls had to get out of bed to feed them. Maria could not imagine why her mother did not step in and protect the girls. She thought it would have been much better if her mother had taken a strap or whip to the boys when they were young, but her mother never did and the boys grew up demanding, rough and rude. Maria's mother never pushed back against the boys. Maria didn't know if her mother submitted to her sons' behavior as a way to appease their father who doted on each of the brothers, or was just so exhausted from the endless work of the cleaning and cooking she had no strength to react to the boys' meanness. Maria's mother, clearly scared of her sons and husband, retreated into constant praying and mindless housework. The woman thought that if her family made it to Church most Sundays she had succeeded in her mission as a parent. Maria vowed that if she ever had sons they would do a lot more than go to mass once a week. They would listen to her and pay the price if they did not.

The boys delighted in constant belittlement of everything the girls said or did. The brothers called the girls stupid and dumb. They were particularly hard on Maria calling her ugly and telling her she would die washing their socks because no one would ever marry her with her squat body and fat legs. Maria knew they were right about her looks, but she also knew they were very dumb about her strength. She had more fortitude than they gave her credit for and was constantly thinking of ways she and Appolina could break free of the family prison they inhabited.

Appolina received very different, but still harsh treatment. Because she was pretty and shapely, the brothers told her they would marry her off to the richest old man they could find. The way they discussed "selling" Appolina was cruel. Appolina was often brought to tears hearing their descriptions of the old, sick and rich men in the area who would be willing to turn over wealth to gain a beautiful young wife. Maria tried to tell Appolina it didn't matter what the brothers planned because the village priest would never agree to a marriage Appolina rejected. Appolina was not sure Maria was right because she knew her brothers would threaten her and Maria if they didn't agree with what the brothers decided. They saw

Apppolina as a meal ticket in their old age. As far as the brothers were concerned she was chattel and they could bargain to get the best price for her. As Appolina grew into a beautiful young woman, her brothers became more excited about the prospects for her, continually discussing which man in that part of Italy would be the best "catch" for the family.

Maria especially hated how their oldest brother, Edwardo, treated Appolina. Edwardo held the most sway with their father. He joined in the brothers' conversations about how to get the best "deal" for Appolina, but also acted like he had rights to her. He stared at her breasts, touched her arms and shoulders and rubbed her back. If she pulled away, he pulled her back. If she protested, he hit her. Maria tried to protect Appolina, but Edwardo told her to mind her own business. Maria looked to her father for help, but none was there. Her father always thought Edwardo was amusing and often laughed when Edwardo pushed against Appolina or held her tight. Maria was frantic to protect her sister and told Appolina she would discuss Edwardo's behavior with her mother. Appolina thought this would be useless, or worse, given what a timid person their mother was, but Maria said she had to try and maybe her mother would understand. After all, how could a mother not notice that her son was inappropriate around her daughter. What mother wouldn't want to protect her daughter? Maria decided to speak to their mother the next day while they were washing her brothers' clothes.

"Mama, I am worried that Edwardo is talking about marrying Appolina to some horrible old villager. Our father seems to agree with him and I don't think the men they are talking about are very nice."

"This is none of your business. You are not Appolina's parent."

"Neither is Edwardo."

"Edwardo is her older brother. He will have a say in what happens. After your father, Edwardo is the man of the house."

Maria was horrified. Her mother was agreeing with Edwardo about Appolina.

"Mother, please, you must see that Edwardo is not always a nice man. He is not thinking about Appolina, he is thinking about himself."

Maria will never forget her mother's expression as she pulled her hand back and slapped Maria's face.

"You must never say horrible things about your family. Edwardo goes to church most Sundays. He is a good man. I did not birth bad children. You have a filthy mind."

Maria was stunned. She thought she was saving Appolina, but her own mother was telling her to back off and accusing her of being the bad person. She was speechless, but she was also mad. She talked to her mother to try to help Appolina but all she accomplished was making her mother furious. Maria tried once more, pleading with her mother to speak to her father about Edwardo's treatment towards Appolina but Maria's mother just shrugged and said that would never happen, it was not her place to speak to her husband about his eldest son. Their father wanted the house to be clean, his food to be cooked and his clothes to be washed. The girls were needed to do the work but had no say in what their father decided. Their mother was not going to risk his anger by interfering. Maria was horrified. Her mother would never help or protect them no matter what her father or brothers did. Maria resolved to take matters into her own hands. She continued to do her work in the house, but the situation with her mother was not good. A coldness settled between them that Maria took as betrayal. She was not sure she would ever be close to her mother again.

There was not much to life in the small village of Bergano in Northern Italy where they lived. The town offered very little schooling and no prospects. If any man could work at the marble quarries, he did. If a man didn't want to do backbreaking quarry work breathing dust and hauling rocks, he usually left the town. The typical exit was to the main coastal road that led to Genoa. There was a bus that ran up and down the coastal road that was the only way to travel so far without a horse. From Genoa ships moved immigrants to America at a steady stream. America sounded like a dream, but Maria could not imagine leaving her village and her country forever. It was alright to dream, but it was a dream that had some pitfalls along with the magic of a new life without her horrible father and brothers and spineless mother. Maria heard of men saving for years to pay the passage to America which equated to about one third of an annual quarry salary. She had managed to save a few lira over the years, but certainly not enough to pay for a way out of the village and certainly not enough to even consider going to America. And maybe that was as it should be. She was an insignificant young woman from a small village in northern Italy. She was not even sure she would like to live in a place she knew nothing about like America. As things got more difficult with Edwardo and the family, Maria frantically thought about something she could do to help her sister and herself, but the normal out for so many Italians of emigrating to America, was not an option.

Her brothers cut a large swath through the town and people of the village were aware of the tension in Maria's family. Some people avoided her brothers because they were so difficult and pushy. Others who wanted nothing to do with Maria's family were often drawn into their horrible actions. The brothers baited people and drank too much. Their idea of fun was any evening that ended in a fight, either with others or each other. They were the town bullies and many people complained to the constable and priest but the boys' father refused to hear that they were out of control. He always shrugged and said they were just boys. Edwardo's bad behavior surpassed his brothers' actions. He hounded every young woman in town and often tried to force his way on them. There were more than a few fights as family members told Edwardo to stay away from their sisters or daughters. Edwardo showed no remorse. He bragged endlessly about how tough and smart he was and told everyone what was wrong with their life. No one liked him.

Maria had a few very good friends in Bergano. Over the years she had become close with a young farmer and his wife who lived at the edge of town. When she had a few free hours, she would visit their farm and share a cup of tea. They worked hard but clearly enjoyed each other, which was wonderful for Maria to see, a happy family, so unlike her own. She also spent time with a group of women, mostly unmarried, who met in the square on mild evenings to share stories, laughter, and their problems. At first, they were careful around Maria, wary because so many of them disliked her brothers, especially

Edwardo. They didn't want to hurt Maria's feelings by talking about her family. But Maria shared with them how horrible the brothers were in their home, so the girls felt free to say what they thought. Some of the girls even spoke of problems in their families. Maria always came away from these conversations feeling she was not so very alone in the world.

One issue she never brought up with her friends was the "selling" of Appolina. She was so distraught about it that she was sure if she mentioned it someone in the village would say something and word would get back to her family. She thought her brothers might kill her if their plan was stopped.

Appolina also had friends in the village, mostly from her few years at school. But Maria noticed that there was one young man, Roberto Feola, who paid special attention to Appolina and Appolina paid special attention to him. Roberto came from a quiet family of stone workers, but unlike his brothers and his father, Roberto had decided to try another occupation, and unlike Appolina's family where going into the quarry to work was a badge of honor, Roberto's family didn't seem to mind that he choose a different path. He had two brothers and two sisters. His parents were very nice and well liked in the village. Maria thought Roberto was a good person and was happy Appolina had a nice friend.

Appolina didn't say much to Maria about Roberto, but she wanted to. She and Roberto were in love. They had found each other in this dusty, boring town, and shared every thought and wish for the last two years. They had been very clever about town gossip, but lately, Appolina knew that people had noticed how often they were together, their heads bent in conversation, looking only at each other. Appolina did not want to anger Maria by hiding her feelings for Roberto. Appolina wanted to be the one to tell Maria how she felt about Roberto. Appolina thought Maria would say they were too young to know what love was, but a conversation with Maria had to happen sometime soon, because Appolina was sure she and Roberto should be together. Roberto was the man she wanted to spend her life with. Because Roberto did not work in the local marble quarry like his father and his two brothers, he had to find another job or leave the village. Roberto surprised his family as well as himself when he started a repair business that was going very well. He could fix wagon wheels, farm implements, household items and complete small building repairs. Until he started this business no one realized how many doors in the town didn't shut properly, how many tools needed to be sharpened after being neglected and stacked in sheds, how many barn roofs needed patching and how many wives were happy to give Roberto a few lira to fix their sagging kitchen shelves rather than pester their husbands about doing the job.

The best part of Roberto's business was that he could come and go as he pleased each day. No one knew where he was going to be working and how long he would be at each place. This gave him great freedom to meet Appolina as she did her daily chores. They set up a schedule that Roberto could rely upon. Appolina went foraging for herbs and nuts in the hills and forest on Monday mornings. She did her family's errands in the town on Tuesdays. She went to the local stream to do wash on Wednesdays. Roberto knew each path, trail and road she used for these outings and they managed to see each other most days of the week. When they met, usually for a half hour at a time, they talked about what was going on in the village and in their families. Lately they spent a great deal of time discussing how they could be together forever. Their meetings were carefully timed and the places planned to avoid most of the people in the area, but every now and then someone came by and they found themselves hiding behind bushes, rocks and trees to avoid being seen. They had been lucky so far, but Appolina was worried it wouldn't last. That is why she wanted to tell Maria what was going on. She knew it would be worse for her sister to hear whispers about her and Roberto from the local gossips. Appolina decided it was time to tell Maria she and Roberto were making plans to be married.

The one thing Appolina never shared with Roberto was the constant conversation in her home about who the brothers could find for her husband. Appolina knew that Roberto would be very angry at her brothers and push her to leave her family. Appolina understood that leaving might be the only way to get away from Edwardo and his plans but she was not ready to leave Maria, who she truly loved. As per custom, Roberto would want to address her father and ask for her hand. Appolina knew he would be rejected and then the situation would be ugly, both for Roberto and Appolina in the town and for Maria and Appolina in the house. Appolina could almost hear her father railing about how Roberto and his family were useless and insignificant. How he would never allow one of his daughters to marry into such an unimportant family. Appolina couldn't imagine the insults her father and Edwardo would shout to everyone about her wonderful Roberto and his lovely family. It would be painful to watch. Roberto's parents would say they could never be associated with a family as vicious and insulting as Appolina's. The whole thing would end in disaster. Appolina had to stop thinking about it or she would cry.

And then things got much worse. One Thursday afternoon, the girls were baking bread for the coming weekend when they saw a quarry runner coming to the house. Maria's mother ran to the door to see what was happening and the girls saw their mother slump to the ground and begin to wail. Maria knew this was bad news. Runners were only used in case of accident or death. Maria braced for the worst. Their father had died in an accident at the quarry. The girls looked at each other with horror. "Edwardo was now in charge." They clung to each other not knowing what to do. Their mother took to her bed, wailing and weeping without stop. Their brothers gathered at the kitchen table, ordered the girls to bring them food and wine and then ordered them to leave. Maria and Appolina were terrified.

Their father was buried in the church graveyard four days later. The brothers all fought about what size tombstone their father should have. Even in the face of tragedy they were most interested in starting a fight. The wake and funeral reception was a nightmare of drinking and shouting. Maria and Appolina were exhausted from putting out food and trying to keep the house in order. Their Mother emerged from her bedroom when the priest arrived to move the body to the church for the funeral mass. Maria watched her father's casket lowered into the ground and thought only of how terrible things could get now that Edwardo was the man of the house. She wished she could feel sorry for her father's death, but she felt almost nothing good about him for so long that it was hard to gather any grief at his passing. She and Appolina looked stricken at the funeral and burial, but it wasn't over the loss of their father, it was fear over the coming changes in the house with Edwardo in charge.

Normal mourning in Italy was one year for the widow and immediate family, but Edwardo began talking about a husband for Appolina within a week of the funeral. Maria said he couldn't do it. The mourning period had to be observed and she threatened to go to the parish priest to stop him. Edwardo just smiled at her and said that arrangements could be made that would take place as soon as the year was over. Maria looked to her mother for help, but her mother just looked down at the floor. There was no way she was going to take on Edwardo now that her husband had passed on. Maria felt trapped.

That night Maria and Appolina took a walk towards the village center. Maria started the conversation,

"Appolina, we have to get away from the village. Edwardo is going to start negotiating for your betrothal and once he starts it will be very hard to stop what he does. Not to mention how angry the man will be who thinks he has bargained for a young bride and finds out you will not agree. And just think of what the house will be like when all of that happens.... It will be hell to live there."

Maria put her arm around her sister, hoping to give her comfort as she delivered this awful decision. She leaned her head towards her younger sister and spoke softly into her ear.

"I think we should plan on sneaking out and finding our way to Genoa. I have enough money for the bus to take us if we get to the main coastal road. When we are in Genoa we'll try to find work and maybe some church will help us. I know it is scary, but if we don't do something we're going to get stuck here forever. You will be married to a horrible old man and I will be a slave to our brothers until I die. Or unless Edwardo kills me first because I refuse to do his bidding."

Appolina put up a hand to stop her sister's monologue.

"Maria, dear, you do not know everything that is happening."

Maria turned to her in surprise,

"What do you mean? There's more than our ugly brother's plans for you?"

"Yes", it was said in almost a whisper.

Appolina took a big breath and tried to steady her voice.

"Maria, I love Roberto Feola and we are planning to be married. He is working out a way to have us go to America. Maria, please believe me when I tell you I love him and he loves me. He is a good and decent person and his family likes me. I never told him about Edwardo and our father planning to marry me off for money, but I am going to tell him now and see if he can help us get away quickly.'

Appolina seized Maria's hand and turned her to face her. She looked directly into her sister's eyes and in a hurried voice continued,

"Maria, will you come with us? I know this is your home and leaving will be hard, but I cannot think of a better plan. If we go only to Genoa, Edwardo will track us down. He will drag us back here and never forgive us for running away and embarrassing him. If he finds out about Roberto and me he will go crazy and hurt or kill him. If he knows we've gone with Roberto, he will hound the Feola family here in the village."

Maria was too stunned to reply at once. When had all this happened and how had she been so blind to not see what was going on? She knew Appolina was right about Edwardo's anger, but could she agree that Appolina and Roberto should decide with no input from their families that they were going to be married, and then go to America? It was almost too much to take in. She motioned for Appolina to sit with her on the rocks forming the bank of the roadside. Maria needed time to think.

"Appolina, what will Roberto's parents say about all of this? Do they know what you are both planning?"

"No, but Roberto is ready to tell his father. Roberto has a cousin who went to America and started a new life. The Feola family talks about what it would be like to go to a big city like the cousin describes in his letters. They wonder what it would be like to live in a place that isn't made up of the local village, the local quarry and the local parish. Roberto says his mother and father will never leave the village, but he thinks his father would not object to one of the sons trying a new life. They are a very close family. Roberto thinks his father would help one of the boys go to America and report back if it is a good option for the others. He even thinks his father would help with the cost of the transport and some living."

"What about your marriage? Do Roberto's parents think that is a good idea? Do they even know?"

Appolina looked worried,

"I think they would agree, but Roberto thinks we should not tell them until we've left. He's afraid his parents would be blamed by people like Edwardo for stealing their sister and ruining her reputation. It would reflect badly on his own sisters when they were ready to marry. Roberto thinks we should go separately and meet in Genoa. He wants to be married on the boat and then tell his parents he has a wife after we reach America. I think it might even be a good idea if he doesn't tell them it is me. That way no one in the village can link Roberto with me and you. As far as our family is concerned I don't care if they know if we are alive or dead. Just that we are gone."

Maria marveled at how much Appolina and Roberto had thought this out. But, paying one passage to America was very different from paying three passages.

"Appolina, maybe you should go and I will stay behind. We'll put all of our money together and I'll steal some from Edwardo over the next few weeks to pay for your passage. I don't think we could ever find enough to pay for both of us."

"Oh no,' Appolina said, 'the only reason I would go is if you were with me. You see I love you and want you with us, but also, you would also be my chaperone. If anything went wrong, no one could say I was compromised with Roberto. If we were caught together before we were married it would ruin him and me, so, you see, you are our insurance that if, God forbid, everything fails we can still live a respectable life in Italy."

Maria had to smile. Her sister was making perfect sense. For so many years Maria had worried about Appolina and thought she had to take care of her, and here were Roberto Feola and her sister plotting their escape from Bergano with no help from Maria. In fact, Appolina had worked it out much more clearly than Maria could have imagined. She wasn't sure the plan would work, but they had no other plan and when would they ever be sure one would work. Maria thought frantically about all of the problems they could have taking on this long trip, abandoning their families and hoping not to be connected so revenge couldn't rain on Roberto's family from her crazy brothers. It was not a perfect plan and it depended on a lot of parts fitting together, but Maria had to admit, it was better than anything they had thought up so far. She was ready to try it.

"Ok, Appolina,' she said as she hugged her sister, 'I am happy you are to be wed to Roberto and I am sorry we cannot celebrate as we should. But it seems to me the most important thing right now is to speak with Roberto and get the details of this plan together. We have much to do if we are going to make this work and we do not have much time.

Appolina was ecstatic. She had always loved her sister, but never more than this moment. Knowing that they would still be together and that she would have her beloved Roberto as her husband was more than she ever dreamed possible. This was the answer, she was sure. She put her arm through her sister's as they walked happily towards the village center. Appolina's voice was almost singing as she replied,

"Yes, you are right. I will arrange for us to meet Roberto tomorrow. And Maria, thank you for understanding. I was so worried you would object to Roberto and me and say we could never succeed. I know you are worried about Edwardo, but we will think of something. He will not ruin our lives."

The sisters hugged again and turned back to their home. And, in a few days they worked it out. Roberto proved far more cunning and devious than Maria had imagined. She understood why he had built such a lucrative business in just a few years. He had a great combination of intelligence, honesty, hard work and charm. But now he was also driven by rage. He listened to Appolina explain what her brothers had planned for her and he was appalled. Never could he believe a family could treat a member like they were planning to treat Appolina. It disgusted him. If he was ever in doubt about what he was going to do, it vanished on hearing the horrible plan the brothers were plotting. Roberto knew he would have to do something to stop Edwardo from ever following them.

Roberto approached his father about going to Sestri Levantre, a coastal town near Genoa, to talk to someone about expanding his business. He asked his father for a loan so he could set up a small group in Sestri Levantre to do his type of handyman work. Roberto had made good money over the last two years in his business and Signore Feola was pleased Roberto was willing to expand. Roberto was sorry to lie to his father but he vowed to pay his father back and explain what happened. If his father knew the whole story, Roberto was sure he would agree it was the best for all.

Maria went through her brothers' possessions in the house and found more cash than she expected hidden away. Now that she knew just where the money was hidden she could get it easily when the moment came. Suddenly the day to leave was upon them. The girls gave a few of their possessions to Roberto to bring along with him. They took only the clothes they usually wore to work in the house and a warm coat. In the middle of the night Roberto met the girls about a half mile from their home on the road out of town and helped them get to Maria's farming friends. The farmer and his wife agreed to hide the girls in their farm wagon early the next day when they moved their vegetables to the coastal town where they regularly traded. Maria thanked them with kisses and hugs and begged them not to ask questions. The farmer knew enough about Maria's family to stay quiet, and since they made the trip to the coastal town each week, no one would wonder why they did it that day. The girls left the cart before the farmers reached the town and flagged down the first bus going north on the coastal road to Genoa. That morning Maria's mother found a note from Maria saying she and Appolina had risen early and headed high up into the hills to forage for mushrooms which were abundant this time of year. Maria's mother was pleased. It would be a good meal she could make for her boys that evening with the fresh mushrooms, although she hoped the girls wouldn't be too late coming back to the village for her to prepare the dinner.

As night fell, the girls had not returned. Edwardo and the boys were greeted by their frantic mother when they came home from work and immediately set out with torches to find if there had been an accident in the hills while the girls were mushroom gathering. They searched until midnight but found nothing. The boys vowed to continue the search at daylight and planned to ask some of the locals to help them.

Roberto planned to leave for Sestri Levantre the next day. Along with most of the men in the village, his brothers and father offered to help with the search for the girls, but Roberto had committed to the meeting with backers in Sestri Levantre and needed to go. He apologized to Maria's brothers, and wished them luck. They said they understood and wished him luck with his business. Each of the search party said goodbye to Roberto and headed towards the hills. About five minutes after the search group left, Roberto slipped a thin wire about six inches from the ground between two door jams along the opening to the barn where the search party had gathered. He piled a small stack of wood just beyond the door inside the barn. He saw that Edwardo hung back, trying to see how the group fanned out as they entered the wooded hills. Roberto called out to Edwardo to come see something in the barn. Edwardo was confused, he thought Roberto had already left. He glanced at the men moving further and further away from him but turned towards Roberto to see what he had found that was so important. Roberto told him to hurry. Edwardo began to run towards the barn so he could see why Roberto called him and still catch up with the men in the search group. As his foot hit the wire, he catapulted forward and landed with his head in the wood pile. He was either unconscious or dead. Roberto waited a moment and then felt for Edwardo's pulse. He was dead. Roberto carefully removed the trip wire and left through the back door of the barn. No one was around and no one saw him leave the barn. As far as anyone would know, he had left for his meeting almost an hour ago. He felt strangely satisfied. And he vowed never to tell Appolina or Maria what had happened in the barn that day.

Roberto met the girls at the dock in Genoa. They timed their departures from Bergano for a sailing Roberto found leaving that day. The cost of the steerage took most of their money and the little they had left they used for food for the voyage. They never looked back. On the second day at sea Roberto and Appolina were married by the ship's captain.

Maria smiled as she remembered giving her bunk to Roberto so the newlyweds could have a wedding night. That turned out to be very fortuitous, because sitting up all night on deck she began to talk with a quiet, calm man named Vito Russo who was headed to America to meet his brother who had left Italy the year before. Vito was a man of average height with kind brown eyes and lovely thick hair. He wanted to know all about Maria, and she found herself unburdening years of anxiety as he nodded, shook his head and smiled, depending on what portion of her miserable life she was relating. He said very little. At the end of the night he took her hand and kissed it. He told her all would be well in America and she believed him. After 14 days on board it was clear that Vito wanted Maria for the rest of his life.

As Maria sat in her kitchen, desperate to get her Danny to be the man she knew he could be, she remembered how insurmountable it seemed to be able to escape her village and toxic family life in Italy. But she and Appolina had succeeded. If she could do that impossible feat, why couldn't she help Danny straighten out his life? She sobbed in despair.

# December 10, 1946 – NORA

D anny Russo sat at a table in a dingy bar/restaurant in Wallingford, Connecticut with his two brothers, Tommy and Frank. As usual, the brothers were arguing, each hoping Danny would intervene and say one of them was right. They always vied for Danny's attention. It was sad that his brothers were so desperate for his approval but Danny had been in this situation hundreds of times over the years with his brothers. He was used to it. Frank was 2 years older than Danny and sweet but basically hopeless. Tommy, at 4 years younger than Danny was the youngest in the family and most volatile of the siblings. Danny, born Dorando Antonio Russo, to Vito and Maria Russo, was always in charge. He could not remember a time when he did not determine what his brothers would do and when they would do it. They always listened to him. That would be very important considering what Danny had in mind for the night.

The three bothers grew up in the rough part of working Wallingford with their 2 sisters and parents in a small, three bedroom, six room house, on a nondescript street. Their father, Vito Russo, worked in the local mill which made bedding for sale to large stores. Vito hardly ever spoke. He deferred all decisions to his wife, who ruled the roost. In fact, Maria Russo might have been the only person Danny was ever afraid of crossing. She seemed to know instinctively when the boys were getting into trouble and was quick to beat them if they were caught. Luckily for Danny, he was very good at school, so she had no cause to be rough with him about his grades or school work. School work aside, Danny managed to get into lots of other trouble, like shoplifting at the Woolworth's in town and hotwiring a car for a joy ride that ended in a ditch. Danny luckily got away before the police arrived, but Maria found out about it and almost broke her arm beating him with a strap. Danny took the beating and figured he had gotten off easy. What were a few sore spots on your back and buttocks compared to being penned in a jail cell? Of course, he might have been able to talk his way out of trouble and get the cops to lay off. He would never know. But he thought it was possible.

Frank and Tommy had their share of trouble too. Frank was caught drinking at age 14 and Tommy tried to run a card game in the basement of the house when he was 16. Maria went crazy over both incidents and the strap came out again. The worst experience for both brothers was getting through the Catholic school curriculum. Frank was slow at school work and would always struggle with studies. Danny thought his mother should leave Frank alone. It was obvious Frank could only do so much. Maria wouldn't let up. Frank had more than his share of beatings each time a nun called Maria to say Frank wasn't applying himself. All Danny could think was, "Fat chance Frank would ever apply himself at school."

Tommy, on the other hand, was bright but couldn't care less about doing the work. Danny told Tommy he was stupid because it was easier to do the work to avoid their mother's wrath when the nuns complained. But Tommy wanted to show he could stand up to the teachers, the principal and his mother. He thought it was funny if he didn't finish homework or prepare for exams. He acted like the teachers reporting his lack of application to his parents was a joke. He thought it made him look important. His payoff was regular beatings by Maria.

The sisters, Anita and Anna, were like nonentities. They were older than the boys and towed the line at school and at home. They very rarely angered their mother. The boys ignored the girls and the girls had no use for their brothers. Both sisters married young and began families. Their freedom from their mother was assured when each of them moved with their husbands more than 100 miles from Wallingford. It was no surprise that both sisters seemed very happy to have their own homes and their own families. They might have gotten along with their mother when they lived at home, but Maria was still a very dominant person in their lives. Other than visits for holidays, the sisters were happy to have their own lives and run their own families. Danny thought they had been clever about getting away.

As the brothers got older, their antics got worse. Once when Tommy was 18 he got drunk and tried to steal a car. The police caught him breaking into the sedan on a street in downtown Wallingford. Tommy panicked when the officers arrived. He tried to punch one of them to get away. Luckily Tommy's wild punch missed hitting any of the police. Two cops dragged him roughly to the squad car. Danny happened to answer the phone in the house when it rang. His first instinct was to hide the call from Maria and his second instinct was to head to the jail as fast as he could get there. He managed to make up a story about the call and then headed out the door. Maria smelled a rat but wasn't sure what was going on.

Danny stopped at the best liquor store in Wallingford on his way to the station and bought whiskey and a few cigars. When he reached the station, the officers were laughing about how pathetic Tommy's attempt to slug them had been. Danny immediately joined in the laughter and told them he was Tommy's guardian. Danny explained that Tommy had been very upset over some family problems, including both his mother and father being very ill. The officers were listening and wondering where this was going. Danny pulled out the bottle of whiskey and the cigars and told the policemen he was very sorry his younger brother had been acting "crazy". Danny said Tommy and his mother were very close and this illness had just devastated him. Danny wasn't sure if they bought the story, but he was sure they were interested in the whiskey and cigars.

One of the policemen told Danny to leave his packages behind and he'd show him to his brother's cell. Danny quickly put the goodies on the desk nearest him and followed the officer to the cell block. Tommy was laying on the cot in the cell looking very drunk and miserable. Danny had a moment's hesitation about getting Tommy out so soon. Maybe a night in jail would both sober him up and get him to straighten out. But Danny also knew that Tommy would not know the story Danny had given the cops. It was going to be tricky if the officers asked any questions. Danny thought it would be better to get Tommy out of the station while he was still drunk so at least anything Tommy said could be chalked up to the booze.

About 30 minutes later, Danny helped a very drunk Tommy walk out of the station. The officers were specific that they were trusting Danny to be sure Tommy didn't get into trouble again. Danny thanked them all and said he really appreciated their understanding. He told them he would never forget them. Once again, the Russo brothers had dodged a bullet.

The next day Tommy was nursing a huge hangover and telling Maria he thought he had the flu. She was skeptical, but Danny acted like Tommy was telling the truth, so she let it go by this time. Danny waited for Maria to go shopping and laid into Tommy. Danny told him how stupid he was and if he ever did anything like trying to hit a police officer again, Danny was through with him. Tommy would be on his own. All of Maria's beatings had not made Tommy consider how he acted, but having Danny threaten to desert him shook Tommy to his knees. He told Danny he would never get into that kind of trouble again. Danny said words were easy, the only way he would believe Tommy was if it never happened again. As far as Danny was concerned, Tommy was on notice from here forward.

That afternoon, Danny visited the upscale liquor store again, purchasing another bottle of whiskey and a few more cigars. That night he headed to the police station and found the same officers he had dealt with the night before at their desks. As he walked towards the officers he put on his most serious face and brought out his mournful look. He said he had come by to thank them again and tell them his mother had taken a turn for the worse. He didn't know how long she had, but he did know how important it was for her to have Tommy by her side. He wanted to let them know how much they had done for the family the night before. The cops looked at each other and nodded their heads. Sometimes it was good to break the rules. They also saw the bottle and cigars Danny laid on the desk as he left. They were happy to know that Danny Russo was such a good guy. And they enjoyed the liquor and cigars immediately.

The household was calm for a while after Tommy's incident, but there was a constant undercurrent of the boys' activities that had Maria and Vito on edge. Both parents hoped they sons would grow out of their antics. Vito was more honest with himself about the boys' behavior than Maria was. He knew a lot was happening in his home, but just shook his head. He worried about Frank and Tommy, but strangely, he was most scarred about Danny. Danny was too smart for his own good and would get himself in trouble with his cocky attitude. Vito couldn't describe why he felt so uneasy about Danny, but he had seen enough men in his life start as very smart young men only to end up as very sad older men. He hoped it wouldn't happen to any of his boys, but the most troubling to him was Danny.

The boys were all grown now, in their 20s and 30s. School was a thing of the past, but Maria still ruled the roost. Frank and Tommy had girlfriends and talked about getting married and moving out of the house to avoid Maria's constant lectures about their bad jobs and lack of initiative. Frank, as the oldest, was particularly embarrassed that he was still home. Tommy spent his free time swaggering around town and talking big about how important he was. Neither of them had any great ambition or initiative but both idolized Danny. Whatever Danny did was the best and whenever they could be with

Danny they hung on his every word. Danny surprised Vito by getting a good job and holding onto it. When Danny was promoted Vito thought maybe his son had finally found his way in life. Now if only Danny could mature into the man Vito hoped he would be. Vito never mentioned he was surprised Danny held his job and was promoted. He just prayed to God that it would last. The place Danny worked was a small tool and dye factory, and Vito had to admit Danny was doing well. Maybe Vito's fears were misplaced. He certainly hoped so.

Maria spent her time cooking and criticizing her sons. Danny realized nothing had changed since they were young and in school, but he was still afraid of Maria's wrath and tried to appease her whenever possible.

Unfortunately, Danny made an enormous blunder when it came to keeping his mother happy. About four years ago Danny met and impregnated a nice Italian girl who lived in Wallingford, Nora Gamino. Nora was 18, sweet, and kind of pretty in a fleshy, Italian way. Her great appeal was she was willing to have sex. Lots of sex. Nora told Danny on their first date that she thought he was wonderful. She smiled up at him and asked if he had ever been with a girl before. He said yes, and she told him she was so glad because she didn't really know what to do and hoped he could show her the right way to make love. Danny couldn't believe his ears. Most girls wanted you to talk with them, take them out for a few dates, and then slowly begin the process of kissing, petting and acting like you cared before anything happened. Nora seemed much more anxious to get on with the good stuff. Danny took her to a secluded part of the Wallingford high school grounds where no one would see them, laid his jacket on the grass, had her lay down next to him and began to kiss and touch her. Danny couldn't believe her reaction. She immediately began to pant and pull at his clothes. In seconds they were both naked and even more quickly Nora was on top of him, gliding his cock into her pussy. She was very wet. Danny held her hips and began to furiously fuck her. Her breasts bounced back and forth as she rode him and within minutes he erupted into her. She slumped down on his chest and heard his heart pounding. She smiled and after a few minutes she said they should get dressed so no one would see them. As they were putting on their clothes she asked him what he was doing the next night. They saw each other nonstop for 6 weeks.

Danny loved to screw Nora and never considered she might get into trouble.

In all of Maria's yelling at her children she never made a reference to the taboo of premarital sex. Of course, the boys talked about sex all the time, but Danny thought mothers depended on their daughters to be careful when it came to babies. His sisters had made it to the alter before having children. He assumed all girls would know how to avoid getting pregnant. It wasn't his problem. As far as Danny was concerned, Nora was responsible for not getting herself knocked up. He never thought to ask her what she was doing given that they were having continuous sex. Little did he know how much trouble this could be.

It still made him strangely nauseous when he thought about the day Nora and her parents came to the Russo house and asked to speak with Vito, Maria and Danny. The six of them, three Gaminos and three Russos sat nervously in the Russo living room, wondering who would start and where was this going. Nora's father began by explaining that Nora was pregnant, there was a child to consider and Danny was to blame. The eruption from Maria was not to be believed. She went insane, screaming at Danny about how stupid he was and vowing to make him marry Nora because she was the mother of his child. Vito shook his head sadly. Danny was in shock. The Gamino family demanded a wedding. Danny looked at Nora to see if she would object to a wedding. They had never spoken about a life together and Danny certainly never considered Nora as a wife. In fact, she would be the last person he would want to marry. He thought she was dumb. It was insulting to him. Unfortunately, Nora seemed perfectly happy to get married. After all, she was going to have Danny's baby.

The wedding took place 4 weeks later. In Wallingford's Italian Catholic community you didn't get a girl pregnant and then walk away. Danny thought he could avoid the marriage but that didn't work out. Danny was threatened with losing his job, paying endless money to Nora for the baby and his family disowning him. It was a nightmare. He was sure he had so many other things to do in life that didn't include a wife and child around his neck when he was just getting started. He wanted to make money, live well and marry a beautiful woman who he could have sex with whenever he wanted. Instead, at age 27 he was headed for a life of drudgery with a woman who he had no feelings for, or worse, hated. And, it infuriated him when he figured out exactly what Nora had done. She knew she wasn't bright or headed for any great future, so she trapped him into marriage to secure her life. She had outwitted the smart guy and he would never forgive her for it.

Nora and Danny's rushed wedding was a somber affair. Danny said, "I do", but didn't mean it. The night they moved into their small, cramped one-bedroom apartment, the shouting began. And it got steadily worse. Nora was still willing to have sex, but Danny was repulsed. He couldn't believe he had been so stupid. He realized he would have to come up with some solution as he watched his wife get bigger and bigger with the pregnancy. He began to tell her he had to take business trips so he could avoid being in the house with her, and gave her money for things she wanted to buy on the condition that she not complain to his or her mother about how they were getting along. He didn't need his mother screaming at him each time they saw each other.

Danny also started to see other women. It was so much easier to be with someone else than with Nora, "the dimwit," as he called her. He realized Nora was clueless when it came to his comings and goings. He met a woman in a bar in North Haven, about 20 minutes away, and sweet talked her into inviting him to her apartment. She was blond and had great tits, so he spent as many nights as he could with her. After a few weeks, she started asking him about his family and his future. He immediately stopped seeing her.

After that incident he was careful to only see a woman two or three times before disappearing. He would pick a woman up in a bar or restaurant, use her home or a motel for some fast, hard sex and ask for her telephone number. He figured that asking for their number always made them feel there was a future and made his leaving easier. He always threw away the number before he got into his car. Whenever he was with someone he always left early enough to get home for a few hours of sleep, a shower and go to work on time. Nora was usually sleeping when he returned, which was fine with him. If he wanted to see a woman for the entire night, he'd leave Nora a note in the morning that he had another business trip and would be gone for the night. This arrangement went on for a few months with Nora apparently none the wiser. But Nora was getting tired of the part time husband she had. One morning after he had been away for about 3 days, she confronted him about never being home. He said he was working as hard as he could to get a raise before the baby was due. He offered her more money if she didn't mention his traveling and being away to their families. He was still worried his mother would see what he was doing and come after him with a vengeance. Nora seemed doubtful but was happy to have more money to spend on baby clothes. Danny thought talking to Nora was like dealing with a ten-year old child who only wanted money to go to the candy store. But he knew this charade couldn't last. There was a baby coming and he would have to figure out how to avoid the apartment and handle Nora going forward.

Nora gave birth to a healthy baby boy. She wanted to name it Henry after her father and Danny didn't care. He tried to put up a good front as a caring father and husband while the families were visiting the newborn, but he could see that his mother and Nora's parents were going to be around a lot more with Henry to gush over. Within days it was obvious that either Nora's mother or Danny's mother would be at the house every day. They both doted on Henry and begged Nora to go out so they could babysit their grandson. Danny saw his mother or in-laws practically every day when they were visiting or taking care of Henry. It was getting harder and harder for him to act like everything was wonderful. It was one thing to be upbeat and jolly every now and then for a family get together, but this daily stuff was exhausting. Eight weeks after Henry was born, Danny got a reprieve. His small tool and dye company was purchased by a larger company, Penn Manufacturing. Danny was told he could interview for a job at Penn. He jumped at the chance. Not only was this a bigger operation with more opportunities for advancement, but it was in Hartford, Connecticut. Hartford was a much bigger city than Wallingford and a place Danny could enjoy. He told Nora that if he got this job they would have more money but the new company might send him on longer business trips. She was happy to hear he was going to have a more important job that paid more money. She tried to ignore that she would see him less. He was ecstatic.

Danny went to work at Penn Manufacturing and rented a room in a boarding house in Hartford where he could stay when he didn't feel like going home, which was most nights. He made himself go to Wallingford for two days each week so he could see the baby and Nora and give her money. He tried to see his brothers to check on how they were doing, and he always stopped by to visit or spoke with his mother when he was there, as though he had been around all week. He wasn't completely sure Maria was buying this act, but it was obvious that Nora and the baby were being cared for so his mother probably chose to look the other way. The rest of the time he was busy at work and in Hartford where he was making a very nice life for himself. In fact, he was in Wallingford that night to take care of something so his great life in Hartford could really get going.

One week before, Danny was invited by a friend to a Knights of Columbus dance in Hartford. Danny was doing very well at work and feeling like he could step out into some of the Hartford nightlife. He knew he looked prosperous in his new clothes and he was proud of the nice wad of cash in his pocket. The Knights of Columbus hall was in downtown Hartford not far from the State Capitol building. It was a beautiful spring night and Danny called Nora to tell her he had to work late that Friday. He told her he would try to get home by noon on Saturday. She said she was tired and the baby was sleeping so all was well. He was nice to her on the phone because he was in a good mood, but he still hated her.

The Knights of Columbus hall was packed with people drinking, smoking and dancing when Danny and his friend arrived. The women were beautifully dressed in gauzy street length gowns with bare shoulders, tiny waists and big skirts. The women were all smiling and laughing and talking with each other and the men. The music was loud, but the din of voices was louder. These were the most stylish people Danny had ever seen, and he knew he would never have seen the same crowd in Wallingford.

Danny asked his friend where most of these people came from. His friend said that Hartford was a magnet for smart young people. The insurance industry, the airplane industry and household names like Colt Firearms, Underwood Typewriter and Hoover vacuum cleaners were all made in Hartford. These people had great jobs and enjoyed themselves in their free time. Many of them had migrated to Hartford for the job opportunities and nice city life. Danny thought he had walked into a fairy tale.

After a few drinks and talking to people he met, the dancing started. Danny wasn't a very good dancer, but he could
hold his own with a few steps and twirling a girl around a bit.
He danced and laughed with a few of the girls in the room
when he suddenly saw across the way a gorgeous young
woman dancing with a guy who looked like he could eat her
up. Danny wasn't surprised because he thought he could eat
her up too. She was average height, but everything else about
her was not average. She had thick, wavy dark long hair that
settled beautifully on her shoulders. Her face was pale and
heart shaped with large dark eyes and beautiful lashes and
eyebrows. When she smiled, her whole face lit up. She was
wearing a modest dress that accentuated her large breasts
and tiny waist. She had a lovely way of cocking her head when
she talked to her partner, and when he held her for a moment, she threw her head back and laughed. She was the
most intriguing woman Danny had ever seen. He realized he
had a hard on just looking at her.

It took Danny no time to work his way over to her. He patiently waited for the music to stop and walked up to her as
she left the dance floor. She was still talking to her partner as
Danny stepped between them and introduced himself. She
was somewhat taken aback but told him her name was Dee
and introduced him to her partner. The music started and
Danny pulled her gently onto the floor. Dee was surprised,
but Danny was very good looking, and what harm could one
dance do. Dee's former partner was not amused. Danny held
her in his arms and could not believe how wonderful she felt.
Danny had never experienced anything like holding Dee. She
was warm and voluptuous with a beautiful face. He asked her

if she lived near there and what she did. Dee had recently moved to Hartford from New York to be closer to her sister and her sister's family. She had a very good job as an inspector at the Underwood Typewriter factory and lived in a small apartment she had just found. Danny looked down into her beautiful hazel eyes and was enthralled. He had never seen a woman so beautiful and shapely and obviously smart. This was who he should be with, not dumb Nora in Wallingford.

Danny monopolized Dee for the rest of the evening. She tried to slip away to speak to the guy she had been dancing with when Danny interrupted them, but Danny held her hand and got her another drink and told her he had so much to ask her about that she had to stay with him. Dee was intrigued with his persistence. She liked the other guy she had been dancing with who was nice and predictable but he was not nearly as good looking as Danny. So, she let herself be held captive for the evening.

When the party broke up, Dee found her girlfriends to make her way home. Danny stopped her at the door and asked her for a telephone number which she gave him. But, she also told him she was seeing another guy right now, so she didn't want Danny to waste his time. Danny just smiled. He couldn't care less about another guy because he intended to sweep Dee off her feet. He did however, have a small problem in his wife and son and he would need to deal with them very quickly. He was sure he would end up with Dee. It didn't matter what Dee thought. He was going to make this happen.

One week later, here Danny was, in this dingy bar with his brothers, ordering a beer and burger and listening to their endless rattling on about some senseless issue. The brothers were boring, but they would be very useful to Danny that night. The bar was about a block and a half from Danny and Nora's apartment. Danny stopped by the apartment earlier in the evening and had a quick dinner with Nora. He even helped put the kid to bed. Danny offered to make Nora a cup of coffee while she cleaned the dishes. She was touched by his gesture, because he was seldom home for dinner and almost never nice to her when they were alone. While Nora was doing the washing up, Danny slipped a sleeping pill into Nora's coffee. Danny had visited the company doctor during the week and complained that he was having trouble sleeping with all the work on his mind. The doctor had prescribed some sleeping pills but cautioned Danny never to take more than one a night because they could be dangerous. Danny had tried one earlier in the week and it had put him to sleep in less than 20 minutes and kept him asleep for more than 7 hours. He just needed to be sure that Nora would fall asleep and stay asleep for a while. He asked her to sit at the table and tell him how the baby was doing while she drank her coffee. Nora dutifully sat down and began to describe each day and the baby's activities. In about 30 minutes she began to say she was very tired. Danny told her that was fine because she was working so hard taking care of the baby while he was working in Hartford he wasn't surprised she was worn out. Danny helped Nora to their bed. He heard her gently begin to snore and headed out to meet his brothers at the bar.

Danny told his brothers he had just been at the apartment with Nora and the baby. Nora had been tired and told Danny to go see his brothers while she put the baby to bed and had a cup of coffee. Danny also told his brothers that he planned to make a business call in about 15 minutes. He needed to speak with a client on the west coast and was going to use the pay phone outside the bar to make the call. He hoped it would be quick, but it could last about 20 minutes. He told his brothers he would pop out when they ordered the burgers and they should just go ahead and eat if he was tied up on the call. Tommy and Frank were so impressed with Danny's new job in Hartford and how well he was doing, a call to client on the west coast sounded important to them. They both said no problem. They would keep his burger until he was done.

After some talk about Maria and how difficult she was and always had been, the boys ordered their meal and Danny slipped out of his chair to make his call. He left the bar and navigated his way through some backyards towards his apartment building. He had scoped out the quickest way to the apartment from the bar avoiding the sidewalks and streets where someone might see him. He arrived at the apartment in less than 3 minutes. Nora was still snoring in their bed and the baby was sleeping in the crib. Danny checked the apartment windows to be sure they were closed tightly and walked quickly to the stove. On more than one occasion when his parents or Nora's mother had been in the apartment Nora had turned on the gas but did not light the burner. The parents repeatedly told Nora to be careful with the stove. Danny took a towel from the sink and covered his hand as he turned on the burner. He put the towel back and moved to the door. He ran through the back yards and stepped into the phone both putting some quarters into the return money slot. He picked up the receiver, fed the coins into the slots and dialed his client's number. Of course, the client did not answer. Danny put the receiver down again. No one could say he hadn't made a call. He had the phone number for one of his clients in his jacket and he had mentioned to the client earlier in the week that they should talk one evening about an issue with an engine part. Danny walked back into the bar about nine minutes after he left. The waitress was just delivering their order and Danny sat down to eat. He looked at his brothers and said the client hadn't been available, although he had tried to call several times. They asked if that was a problem, but Danny just shrugged and said he would talk to the client another time. They all began to eat their burgers and drink their beers, chatting and laughing the whole time about days gone by and what a dump the town of Wallingford was. They never noticed the sirens from the fire trucks or the ambulance. They stayed at the bar for about two hours.

Danny's wife and son were declared dead of gas asphyxiation. Danny went to the apartment, now surrounded by firemen, ambulance drivers and policemen, a few hours later. One of the officers who had taken Tommy into custody a few years before was there. Danny tried to get into the apartment but the officer restrained him saying there was nothing Danny could do. They had already taken the bodies out. Danny began to cry and talk about Nora being careless with the gas stove. The officer patted his back and said they needed to interview him. Danny agreed. He said he saw Nora and the baby earlier in the evening before meeting his brothers for a burger. Danny told the officer he had been with Tommy and Frank the whole night. The officer asked him if he had left the bar at any time. Danny said he had used the phone booth outside the bar to make a quick business call to the west coast. The officer patted his back again. He asked Danny if his mother had made it. Danny took a second to recall his story at the police station when Tommy had been picked up. He quickly said that yes, she had pulled through and he thanked the officer for asking. The policeman shook his head and said,

"You've had a rough go for the past few years and now this. I am really sorry."

Danny thanked him again.

That night, Danny told his family that Nora and Henry were dead. Maria couldn't believe it. She doubled over in grief and sobbed. She was overwhelmed by the news she just heard. Of all the horrible, rotten things that had gone wrong in her life, she thought this was the worst. She was a tough woman, but this was hard to take. Her only grandson had just died with his mother in a stupid accident. She prayed it was just a bad dream and hadn't really happened, but deep down she knew it had. Maria, who was used to bending everything to her will was powerless. Henry was gone. Maria thought the worst day had been when her smart son... not the slow son, and not the wild son.... had thrown away his future by getting a pathetic, spineless girl like Nora Gamino pregnant. When it was obvious that Danny would have to marry Nora Maria's hopes for her smart son's future were blown away in one painful, sad and depressing moment. Maria remembered the Gaminos, Nora, her father and mother, sitting in Maria's living room explaining that Danny was the father of the child Nora was carrying. Maria wailed and her quiet husband, Vito, shook his head and cried. Danny looked shocked, but that only made Maria angrier. Danny, her smart son, her handsome son, her successful son just brought devastation on the family. The only good to come out of that disaster had been the life of sweet, adorable baby Henry, a true angel God had sent to their family. Maria was beside herself. If only Danny had never gotten Nora pregnant, if only stupid Nora had remembered to turn off the gas, if only.....

The funeral was held the following Saturday. Danny's family and Nora's parents were there with a few close friends. Danny was dutifully sad, but he was also planning his next meeting with Dee.

# December 17, 1946 – DEE

D ee was surprised when she got the call from Danny Russo. She hadn't heard from him for more than two weeks and interested as she was in the tall, dark, handsome Italian guy, she had plenty of other men chasing her. Jack Torry, the guy she was dancing with when Danny appeared at the Knights of Columbus party called her constantly. He was nice enough but somewhat dull. It didn't help that he lived with his mother and checked with Mom's schedule whenever he asked Dee if she had some free time for him. Dee thought she would be happier with a more independent guy. She also wanted to find someone who was successful. Her upbringing had been tough and she wanted to avoid the hardships her family endured raising their children and keeping food on the table.

When Danny called she was pleasantly surprised because she hadn't forgotten about him. When he hadn't called for a few weeks, she tried to put him out of her mind. If he wasn't interested enough to call her, she could get over it. But, she had to admit she was happy when he did call. In addition to Jack, Dee met a at least 4 or 5 handsome men over the eighteen months she had been in Hartford, but without a doubt, Danny was the most good looking of all.

Danny was very friendly and talkative on the phone. He asked Dee if he could see her the next weekend. She had

planned to see Jack Torry that weekend, but Jack was always around, and Dee was getting a little tired of how dull
he could be. She smiled thinking it would turn the tables on
Jack to say she was too busy to see him, rather than him
tell her his mother needed him and he only had a few hours
for Dee. Danny, she thought, couldn't be more different than
Jack. Danny was stronger and more forceful than Jack and for
some reason, having someone so different from Jack seemed
exciting. Dee told Danny she could arrange her schedule to
see him on Saturday.

Dee needed to plan what she would wear and how she
would do her hair for their date. Now that she had a good
solid job at Underwood Company she had built up her wardrobe and could spend some money on the hairdresser for a
special occasion. She was excited about the coming weekend, and she was very happy about the decision she made to
move to Hartford from Brooklyn, NY.

Brooklyn was a fun place to live for awhile but after about
five years it was became boring to be at the beck and call of
the family she worked for as a nanny. She didn't really like
children very much. They got on her nerves. Ironically, to be
around children was one of the excuses she gave her parents
for moving to Hartford. Her older sister, Mary and husband,
George, had three young children and lived in Hartford. Dee
told her mom and dad that she wanted to be near Mary and
the children when she left Brooklyn. Her parents wanted her
to move back to their home in Scranton. Dee couldn't think
of a place she wanted to live in less than Scranton. To avoid
going back to Scranton she told her parents she wanted to be
near Mary and her children. She didn't like children any more

now than when she was 17, but she was sure anything was better than returning to Scranton, Pennsylvania.

Dee's family was made up of her mom, dad, Dee and two sisters. Her parents had both emigrated from Lithuania before the first World War. They spoke no English. Dee was the middle child. Her oldest sister, Mary, was the family darling. Mary was petite and pretty. She did everything right. She was a model student, she was the president of the Ladies Sodality at the church. On and on it went about perfect Mary. Dee was sick of hearing how they should all be like Mary. Her younger sister, Helen, was very smart in school which helped with her standing in the family, but she was a whiner, and nothing ever made her happy. The family rolled their eyes and threw each other knowing glances when Helen took off on one of her "woe is me" tirades. The ranting almost always centered around how no one appreciated her or gave her credit for how smart she was and what a good job she did on her school work. The family ignored Helen whenever they could.

Dee's father, who was a miner, worked hard when he found work, but the mining situation in Scranton was never steady and the family lived a simple life centered around the house, their Lithuanian church and her father's favorite beer garden. Daily life in Scranton consisted of school, housework and gardening which supplied much of the food the family needed to supplement their father's meager income. They also raised chickens and sold eggs to the neighbors. Dee's mother was adept at hand weaving cotton rugs she fashioned from rags and making the girls' clothes as they grew larger. A big family joke that Dee hated was that Mary and Helen's clothes didn't take much fabric, but Dee, who was larger, consumed more cloth for each dress. Helen said that meant Dee should get fewer dresses. Dee didn't think this was funny. There was not a penny to spare in their lives. The family depended on the church for their social activities because there was never enough cash to go to a movie or restaurant. The girls dreaded when their father went to the beer garden on payday because their mother made them go and fetch him home. Their mother was frantic that he would spend too much on drinking and they would be scrounging for food until the next paycheck.

The girls learned English when they started first grade, which was at the parish church school, and tried to get their parents to speak English in the house. This did not go over well. Both parents were proud of their Lithuanian background and although they had left the old country behind, they had no intention of letting their heritage go.

Dee was bored in Scranton and wanted better things in her life. When the depression took away her father's job the two older girls had to pitch in. Mary left high school after two years and worked as a cleaning lady for a rich family in the more affluent part of town. Dee, who also had to leave high school after her sophomore year, found a position through a friend of a friend with a family in Brooklyn that needed someone to live in and help with the children. Dee's mom and dad expected both girls to give their paychecks to their parents. This was never questioned.

Dee thought the chance to go to New York and get away from the drudgery of the slag heaps and unpaved streets of Scranton was a gift. She couldn't wait to say yes to the job, even though taking care of children was not her favorite thing to do. Luckily, when she got to Brooklyn, the mother was more interested in being with the kids than in keeping house. This was fine with Dee. She fell into a routine of doing most of the cooking and the cleaning, and occasionally minding the children when the mother was busy. As expected, both Mary and Dee routinely handed their pay over to their mother. Their mother then returned some "spending money" to them. Sometimes, if any large bills had to be paid in Scranton, the girls got nothing for their weekly efforts.

In 1939 Dee's older sister, Mary, married a guy named George Vitas, a fellow Lithuanian from Scranton who was five years older than Mary and seven years older than Dee. Mary and George met at a church social, and as Dee was sad to admit, Mary again was the perfect child, finding a handsome, interesting guy who was also Lithuanian. Dee agreed with everyone that George would make a solid husband and it was clear Dee's parents loved him. George was older and acted more mature than any of the sisters. Dee saw that her father was especially close to George which she guessed was because her dad never had a son. George supplied another male voice among the female chatter in the house. Dee's father loved the comradery. After the wedding George and Mary moved into the house with Dee's family but Dee knew that wouldn't last long. Within a year George found a great job in Hartford through his cousin who had moved to Hartford the year before and the young couple left Scranton for a new life in New England. Dee's mom and dad were sad to say goodbye to the couple, but George found a Lithuanian church in Hartford they planned to join and the parents were happy

Mary would be among people like them. George promised to bring Mary home to Scranton for visits whenever he could,

After five years with the Irish family Dee decided to leave Brooklyn. She had spent most of the war in Brooklyn and had recently heard stories from some friends about great jobs available to anyone who wanted to work in factories. She had had enough of children and yearned to be on her own. Because Mary and George lived in Hartford moving there was an easy way to avoid going to Scranton. Dee knew what life was like in Scranton, a dead town with dilapidated buildings and sad shopping areas. She had seen some of New York while in Brooklyn and loved it. Scranton didn't measure up to the excitement she craved. She saw it as "going backwards" in life. And although Hartford was no New York, she was ready to go almost anywhere but Scranton. Mary and George, and their children, made the decision all the easier. It was Hartford without a doubt. It helped that Mary and George made the trip from Hartford to Scranton regularly to see their parents. Dee could assure her mom and dad that she would be coming back whenever Mary and George brought the children to Scranton for visits.

The move to Hartford was almost 2 years ago and Dee did not regret her decision. Within weeks of arriving she found a job on the assembly line at the Underwood Company which made typewriters. Everyone said that working for Underwood was a great job. Dee was careful about her work and knew not to make waves. She came to the job with no experience and loved learning anything she could about her new position. She had a long talk with Mary about her paycheck and her parents. Mary said that their mother never asked for money once Mary and George were married. Since Dee, who was living with Mary and George since coming to Hartford needed to get an apartment for herself, Mary told Dee to ask her mother if she could keep her paycheck. Dee was relieved and wrote to her mother that she now needed her paycheck to pay for her apartment and food. Her mother accepted the change in circumstances but made it clear that Dee needed to be careful,

"Mary is married to George and he will provide for her and the children. You are on your own. Don't expect us to help you out if you live beyond your income."

Dee heard the message loud and clear. If she was no longer sending money back to the family in Scranton she could no longer count on their safety net. She was truly on her own. Dee was fine with this arrangement because she was very careful with money and would never put herself in a position where she needed to go begging back to her parents for help. She took it as a source of pride that she could make ends meet on her own.

The paychecks from Underwood were not overly generous but she got one every week. Dee parceled out each purchase she made to be sure she could handle the cost. She ate simply and took a small, very low cost apartment for her lodging. Her building was clean but the apartment was only one room with a small kitchen nook, bathroom and closet. The sofa converted to a bed for her to sleep. She thought it was perfect. She took the bus from home to work each day and always accepted overtime work when it was offered. She spent hours going through sales racks at the department stores in Hartford finding mark downs for clothes she could wear for social events. She was very good at sewing and sometimes found cast offs at the Good Will store that she remade to fit. Within a few months she had shaped a wardrobe which was attractive and flattering. She saw Mary and Andy and their children every week and made girlfriends easily. Things were generally going very well for her in Hartford.

There was one small issue in Dee's life that kept bothering her and, she suspected, it bothered her family too. Dee was 25 years old and unmarried. In the last year her younger sister, Helen, married a young man who returned from the war. His name was Walter, or Wally for short. Although he was from Scranton, he was not the ideal husband. His mother was Lithuanian but his father was Polish he did not speak Lithuanian so he wasn't quite as good as George. After their wedding Helen and Wally moved into Dee's parents' home. Unlike George and Mary, Dee felt this arrangement was going to be permanent. Dee didn't see Wally as a guy with the ambition to relocate and start a new life. She thought Helen and Wally were stuck in Scranton and probably would be there forever. But the issue of Dee not being married with both of her sisters settled bothered her. She wondered when she would meet someone she liked enough to commit herself to a life together. She also thought that at 25 she was in danger of becoming an old maid and that scarred her. Dee's answer to this problem was that whenever she could she went out with friends hoping to meet someone nice. Up to this point there were plenty of guys who seemed interested in her, but other than Jack Torry, who she thought was too much of a milk toast with balding hair and a short, squat body, she had no real serious beaus. Now this Danny Russo had resurfaced and she wanted to see how that would go. Danny was obviously not Lithuanian, but Helen had already broken the mold on that score so maybe it would be OK if this guy worked out.

Dee remembered how Danny had muscled his way between Jack Torry and her at the dance and what it felt like to be held by him. She remembered the way he stared at her face. She knew she wasn't bad looking. She was happy her hair was so nice when so many girls had trouble keeping a wave or avoiding frizz, and she knew she had a nice smile, but Danny acted like she was beautiful. He held her tightly when they danced, and she liked the feeling of him molding his body to hers. He felt strong and it excited her to be near him. She took extra care dressing and putting on the little makeup she wore. She hoped that she looked good enough for him. Danny had been dressed so beautifully when they met that she knew he liked nice clothes and how someone looked would be important to him.

Dee worked out the schedule for the bus ride so she would be on time. She was a little nervous, but happy that this was happening. After all, someone who looked like Danny didn't appear every day. She hadn't mentioned the date to Mary or her friends. This was her adventure and she wanted to see how it worked out before she spread any news about Danny. If it didn't work out she didn't want to have to explain what happened. It was always easier to see if it was going somewhere before talking about a beau than to explain a disaster after just a date or two. This was a safe way to handle this new guy and Dee was glad she was being careful. In her dreams Danny turned out to be a great guy and she could parade him around to everyone. Christmas was the following week and she would be going to Scranton with George and Mary and the kids to see her parents. It would be wonderful if she could tell them all she had met a fabulous guy. She imagined how happy they would all be for her, and how relieved her parents would be. This Christmas might be one of the best ever, especially if she could make this happy announcement. She knew it was very soon after they met, but if tonight went well and she was comfortable with how they got along, she would love the chance to make a big splash when the family was all together. Yes, it would be wonderful. She felt positive about this. She was happy and found herself laughing as she boarded the bus to their date.

# December 21, 1946 – DANNY

Danny was ecstatic to be back in Hartford. The last 12 days in Wallingford had been horrible. He got through the night Nora and Henry died, but the following days getting ready for the wake and funeral were a grind. He couldn't believe how difficult his mother and aunt, Appolina, had been. They wanted him involved in every part of the planning of the service. He couldn't care less what the corpses wore in the caskets or what flowers were from "Beloved Husband" and "Loving Father", as the banner on the carnations and gladiolas covering the caskets said. He just wanted the whole thing to be over as quickly as possible. He thought his mother took his short answers and abrupt decisions as a sign of his despair. He hoped he looked mournful enough when he followed the caskets out of the church and to the cemetery. He was dressed in his best suit with a starched white shirt and dark tie. It was very cold the day they buried his family so he wore a new topcoat he had purchased the month before and a hat and gloves. The best front, he thought, would be to look like a proper widower.

His brothers took him out for drinks the night before the wake, but it was clear they had no idea what to say to him and were afraid of any of their usual topics which were horses, gambling and women. He almost felt sorry for them, but then realized that they were feeling sorry for him. He was annoyed he had to keep up the charade. Getting rid of Nora and the kid were a godsend to his plans. He figured he could bolt from Wallingford on Sunday afternoon after the funeral. He could say that he had to be ready to go to work the next day in Hartford. He missed enough work and he didn't want to harm his job standing by being away too long. He would ask his mother and mother in law to close up the apartment in Wallingford and dispose of Nora and Henry's things. After all, what would he know to do with a bunch of women's and baby clothes. He knew his mother would say yes.

The one thing he couldn't do was cry. It was beyond him. Nora and Henry were a rock around his neck. He never wanted to have this family and Nora had trapped him into the marriage. It was never going to work and as far as he was concerned it was going to end sometime so this was as good a time as any. There were lots of tears at the funeral. Between his mother, aunt and Nora's parents, Danny figured they cried a river. He spent the entire service looking down at his hands in his lap. No one could fault him for not being sad, or at least for not acting sad.

Now he was back at his little apartment in Hartford and he was totally free. He went to work on Monday and accepted everyone's condolences. He learned to say thank you with great sincerity and then followed up with a slow shake of his head and the phrase, "Life goes on". He threw himself into his work and was uncharacteristically quiet in meetings he attended. He thought it was best if he laid low for a few weeks at the office which meant no badgering people for their mistakes, no loud shouting and no obvious gambling. He figured about a month would be enough. The CEO of the place came to his desk to give his sympathy. Danny had the routine down, thanked him sincerely and said he only wanted to do his work to get over the shock. The CEO nodded and patted him on the shoulder,

"Don't overdo it too soon. This has been a terrible thing you are dealing with. If you need time, take it. We know you'll be back and helping us as soon as you can."

Danny looked at him with what he thought was a devastated face.

"Thanks so much. I appreciate it. But, I really think working is the best thing I can do now. I don't have much else to live for."

The CEO gave him a small smile and left. Danny figured it helped him a lot to use the line about working being so important. Someday he could collect on that at the office.

That night he stayed in and went to bed early. The next day he called Dee, chatted her up a bit and asked her to have dinner with him the following Saturday. She accepted after lying about having to readjust her schedule. She probably thought he was worried about her having other guys to see, but he knew better. She was making it up. He could sense that she wanted to see him. He knew he had impressed her and he was sure she was happy to take their relationship further. He felt really good. Dee was the reason he had taken care of Nora and the kid. Now he wanted to see her as soon as he thought it would be acceptable. He picked a restaurant on the edge of the city so there was very little chance he would bump into anyone he knew. If he did see someone he could say Dee was a relative who wanted to lift his spirits after the funeral and asked to have a quiet dinner with him. He was sure this would be fine. He just had to keep up the sad front at work until Saturday when he could be with Dee and away from the drudgery of everyone mentioning the tragedy of this small family, their funeral and burial. He was anxious to get through the next month. He was sure by that time everyone would have forgotten about Nora and he could go back to his regular life style. He would have to slow walk it with Dee until the month was over. It wouldn't be that hard with the holidays coming. He'd go to Wallingford for a day or so for Christmas and then tell his family he had to concentrate on his work and come back to Hartford. He figured it would be best if he skipped a New Year's Eve party to show he was still in mourning. He could tell Dee he always spent New Year's Eve with his brothers and he couldn't disappoint them at the last minute. She would think that was nice. He thought this would all work out just fine.

Danny smiled in the mirror as he adjusted his tie. He was so happy he could look forward to an entire night where no one mentioned Nora or Henry and no one thought they had to speak softly around him. He was ready to rev up his best lines and charm the pants off Dee. He hoped she liked the restaurant and he hoped she wanted to have some real fun afterwards. He didn't intend to tell her he had been married. That information could wait for a very long time. In fact, it could wait forever depending on how it went with Dee. He could use it for sympathy if he needed, but certainly not for a while. The best thing that could happen would be if Dee never found out about the whole Nora affair. That is, never found out unless Danny found a moment when he could use telling the story to his own advantage. After all, it wasn't like he was going to run out and get married quickly again. He knew how he felt about that, and it wasn't for him. From now on, he wanted to enjoy women but have his freedom. He had no intention of getting sucked into marriage again. Dee was just the kind of girl he wanted around. She was smart, self-sufficient and sexy. He couldn't wait to get her into bed. He licked his lips and rubbed his newly shaven face. He felt good. He wondered how Dee looked with only her bra and panties on with her full lush breasts and her small waist and her gorgeous rear end. What a beautiful body she had, her hair was like thick silk and her smile was great. Yes. He was ready for a great night.

# December 21, 1946 – DEE

D ee opened the door to the restaurant. She was freezing. The walk from the bus stop was further than she
expected and she was happy to finally be in the warm room.
She looked around for Danny but didn't see him. She began
to take off her coat as the Hostess approached. Suddenly
she felt hands around her waist. Someone was holding
her from behind. She held her coat to the side and turned.
Danny was behind her smiling down.

"You look gorgeous with your red cheeks and bright eyes.
But your hands are freezing," he said as he took the coat from
her and held her hand. She smiled back at him.

"I forgot my gloves and couldn't hold up the directions to
the restaurant and keep my hands in my pockets at the same
time."

He smiled into her eyes as he lifted her hands to his mouth
and blew on them to warm them up.

"Well, that's my first job of the night. We've got to get you
warmer. The second job is a trip to the stores when they open
on Monday. We need to buy you a pair of gloves."

She pulled her hands back and laughed.

"Don't be silly, I have gloves, I just didn't remember to
bring them."

He looked at her strangely, "It doesn't matter if you have

gloves, wouldn't you want to get a new pair if someone offered them to you?"

She wasn't sure how to respond to this. She thought it was nice that he worried she didn't have gloves, but if you had a perfectly good pair of gloves, why did you need another pair? She came from a family that never bought more than they needed and usually went without until it was a dire situation. She smiled weakly at him and looked around the restaurant.

"This is very nice. Do you come here often?" He lifted his eye brows and looked at her intensely. She thought she had said something wrong.

"Oh, I'm so sorry. I didn't mean to pry. You don't have to tell me how often you come here. I just wanted you to know that it is very nice and it is special and I don't go to that many restaurants, so I don't know much about good ones and bad ones and which are expensive and which aren't...," she realized she was rattling on and probably sounded pretty stupid. Like the hick she was from Scranton.

"No, no no,' he responded, 'I am happy to discuss this restaurant with you. I was just staring at you because you are so beautiful. But you must know that. I would think every man who ever met you has said you are beautiful. Am I right?"

She started to laugh, but then blushed very red. "I think you are teasing me. No, men do not say that when they meet me and I am not sure I've heard that more than two times in my life." She paused and continued, "You can stop saying these things just to flatter me. It's silly. "

"Ok, I'll stop so long as I can look at you." He was smiling as he moved closer to her face.

She waved a hand in the air as if to brush him away.

Based on this beginning, she was completely lost as to what they would talk about all night. So far it had not been comfortable chit chat. Dee was not from a background that threw out compliments and told people they were beautiful. Yes, for special occasions she remembered her mother or father saying someone looked nice, especially if the someone was perfect Mary, but these types of compliments were not the usual conversation she would have with someone who was almost a stranger. She began to wonder if she had made a mistake with Danny. She didn't know where this was going.

The hostess escorted them to a table and Dee sat down. Danny didn't sit across from her, he chose the chair by her side. She looked at him and tried to relax. This was supposed to be fun. Why was she feeling so uncomfortable?

Danny immediately signaled the waiter.

"Would you like a drink? I'm going to have a highball."

She nodded to show she thought would be fine, hoping that a drink would lighten her mood.

Danny seemed to sense that things weren't right. Dee seemed nervous. He leaned back in his chair and started asking her questions about her work and her family. He hoped that getting her to have a drink and talk about herself would make her relax. He couldn't stop staring at her. Her eyes were a lovely shade of hazel, almost honey colored and her body rivaled that of Jane Russell, the famous actress. In fact, Danny thought her body might be better than Jane Russell's. He wouldn't be surprised if every man in the placed was staring at her.

"So tell me how a beautiful girl lands in Hartford and

attends a Knights of Columbus dance on the very day that I go to my first Knights of Columbus dance?"

She laughed at that and began to speak. He was somewhat bored when she launched into the long explanation of her life in Scranton, her job with the Irish family in Brooklyn and then her relocation to Hartford about 18 months ago. She told him about her sister's family living in Hartford and about her happiness at finding a job at Underwood on the assembly line.

"It wasn't easy," she continued, "to have no experience or job skills and land a job in a solid company where the pay is good and the chance for promotion was available." Danny nodded dutifully.

She was so gorgeous to look at, her hair was so thick and her body was so lush he began imagining getting her into bed and the fun that would be. Maybe it would be like when he first met Nora and she was hungry for sex. Maybe it would be even more fun and Dee would beg for sex. That would be a total home run, because unlike Nora, Dee was a full-grown woman and was much more alluring to him than the young stupid girl Nora was when he first fucked her.

Dee paused in her story. She looked intensely at Danny, "and what about you, your family and your work?"

Danny pulled himself away from his fantasies and responded by inventing the nicest version of his upbringing in Wallingford he could muster. He talked about his brothers without mentioning their troubles with the law or lack of initiative, his sisters without mentioning their escape from their mother's hovering, and his parents without mentioning that his mother ruled the family like a tyrant and his father seldom spoke. He explained how he had applied for and won the job in Hartford when his old firm in Wallingford was sold to Penn Manufacturing. He told Dee how successful he was at Penn and how quickly he had been promoted. He hoped to be promoted again soon because he had a knack for finding the best answer to manufacturing problems. The CEO had recently visited his desk to tell him what a great job he was doing.

What he carefully avoided was any discussion of his former wife and child and his first marriage. Danny was pretty sure that Dee would never think to ask about a former marriage or do any digging in the Wallingford area about his early life. She was too unsophisticated to think that way and that was fine with him.

By the time they finished dinner Dee was chatting comfortably with Danny and seemed much more at ease. He found out she had never traveled anywhere outside Scranton but New York and Hartford, and unlike most girls in the post war era, she had never bothered to get her driver's license. Danny thought this was strange. He wondered how she got around and if she missed the freedom of being able to drive. She shrugged and said she was used to going places on her own by bus or with her friends.

After some dessert and coffee, Danny offered to drive Dee home. He was hoping she would invite him into her apartment. Within minutes of parking in front of the building, it was obvious he wasn't going to be seeing the inside. Dee thanked him for dinner and offered her hand for Danny to shake. He was so surprised he just stared at her hand. Then he pulled himself together and pulled off his glove. He took her hand and smiled.

"You are really something, you know. A whole dinner and I get a handshake? I thought the meal was better than that."

Dee looked out the window to her apartment building and back to him.

"Danny, you don't know me after one date. It was fun and I appreciate the dinner and ride home. I liked hearing about your family and your work." Dee seemed to run out of words but didn't take her eyes off him.

Danny leaned over and used his other hand to cup her neck and pull her towards him for a kiss. At first she didn't open her mouth, he played with her lips and then used his tongue to push her lips apart. Dee had a sudden intake of breath and pulled away. Danny pulled her back and she slowly opened her mouth to him. He began to kiss her deeply. She was panting and he pulled her closer. She had no idea what he was doing because she had never done this before, but she loved how it felt. He kissed her cheeks, her forehead and her chin, but kept coming back to her mouth. She felt devoured by him. Finally, she pulled away. They both sat looking forward breathing heavily.

"Can I see you again?", he said.

She waited before she answered. Finally she said, "Yes."

Dee opened the car door and walked on wobbly legs into her apartment building. She climbed the stairs and let herself into her small space. She sat on the sofa bed and thought about the evening. He was gorgeous and he was ambitious. He was doing well at work and he was hoping to do even better. He was interesting to talk to and seemed to be interested in her. Above all, he said over and over how much he liked her. She was not used to this treatment. No one she knew said things like that to someone they had just met. Was she crazy or was this normal? Was she such an old maid that she had no idea how men and women acted together when they were alone? Was the way he kissed her the way you were supposed to kiss? She had never seen people kiss like that, not even in the raciest movie she had ever seen. And, she liked it. It felt wonderful. And he wanted to see her again.

Then a very scary thought hit her. Did she have to go to confession and tell the priest what had just happened?

# January 11, 1947 – APPOLINA

Appolina dropped her shopping bags on the floor of the living room as she entered the house. She was very upset at what she had just seen. Her husband, Roberto, wasn't home and wouldn't be home for a while. He had gone to help a friend with his broken-down car. Appolina didn't know what to do but she knew she had to speak with Roberto before she did anything.

Who knew an innocent trip to do some shopping in Hartford would lead to this dilemma. Appolina was paying a sales girl at G Fox & Company on Main Street in Hartford for a small gift she was going to take to a girlfriend's birthday party when she looked up and across the floor saw Danny Russo, her nephew, with a beautiful young woman. Danny had his arm around the girl and she was pushing him away playfully. Clearly they were close, if not more. Danny was showing the girl a pair of leather gloves and making her try them on. They were laughing. Danny nuzzled the girl's neck. Then Appolina distinctly heard Danny say, "We'll take them. They are for my best girl. I want her to be warm."

Applolina turned away so that Danny wouldn't see her. She took her packages and walked back as far as she could away from the glove counter. She was confused and angry, but mostly she wanted to cry. Less than a month ago, Danny had buried his wife and his child. Appolina had cried as hard as anyone at the funeral. The two white caskets, one large and one small, wrenched her heart. She thought it was the saddest moment of her life. At the funeral Danny seemed distraught, but stoic. He didn't cry, but he seemed shaken. Now to see this, so soon after that nightmare was hard to take. She was confused, but she was also angry. Over the years she worried that this was the "real" Danny. Her sister Maria didn't want to see it, but since he was a child Appolina and Roberto watched Danny, who was endlessly praised by Maria, acting like a very different person than his mother described. They knew Danny was not as perfect as Maria thought.

Appolina reminisced on her long history with Maria and Vito Russo and their children. From the time she and Roberto stepped off the boat from Genoa in New York, Maria and Vito had been their closest family. Maria managed to give birth to five children all of whom lived. Appolina and Roberto were not so lucky. For whatever reason, God determined that they should not be parents. Appolina often thought their childlessness was God's retribution for her running away from her mother and brothers in their village in Italy. Roberto hated when she blamed herself for their childlessness. Roberto assured her it was God's retribution for something terrible he did in Italy before they left. He refused to tell Appolina what it was he did, but he was convinced it was his fault there were no children, not his wife's doing. They loved each other very much and accepted what God had decided for them. They became very close to Maria's children and helped raise the entire Russo brood.

Roberto and Appolina lived in East Hartford in a small,

modest home. Because there were only two of them it was easy to live simply. They had very few needs. When they arrived in Connecticut Roberto found a good job at a growing company called Pratt & Whitney. He had done well working on the burr bench at the factory making airplane engine parts and over the years he slowly advanced to supervisor of his area. Like Danny, Roberto was exempt from military service during the war because he worked in a war related industry. Vito and Maria settled in Wallingford where Vito found work in a mill. The 25 miles between them had shrunk over the years as the roads around Hartford improved and each of them owned cars. They spent every holiday and many weekends together. When the children were younger, Appoliana would appear in Wallingford and help Maria with the housework and cooking. The children treated Appolina and Roberto as part of the immediate family. Because Maria, Appolina and Roberto left their families behind in Italy, they clung to each other.

Over the years, Roberto and Appolina saw how the Russo family operated. The girls were smart and anxious to be married and in their own homes. Appolina didn't blame them, Maria was very strict and demanding. In a way, it wasn't that much different than what happened in Italy. Maria was never as difficult as their mother in Italy had been, acting like the boys were God's gift and the girls were slaves to do the men's bidding. But Appolina understood why a young girl would want to have her own home and her own say in how it ran. In Italy, Maria and Appolina grew to hate their mother and how she treated them both as workhorses. It was true Appolina and Maria left Italy because their brothers were so horrible, but even if the brothers had been nice to the girls, Maria and Appolina would have wanted to get away from their mother and her endless demands. Now Maria's daughters had also left their home, but in America they continued to have a relationship with their mother. They might live far away and run their own homes, but they continued to visit for holidays and stay in touch. Appolina thought Maria and her trip to America had resulted in a much better family situation than they endured in their little village back in the old country. It made Appolina happy she and Maria had the guts to leave Italy those many years ago.

The Russo boys, Tommy, Danny and Frank were another story. Unlike the girls who Appolina thought could take care of themselves now they were married, the boys were not so dependable. Frank was barely able to hold a job and Tommy was always one step away from trouble with the police. Roberto heard that Danny had sweet talked the cops out of charging Tommy with assault, but Roberto guessed that wasn't the only time Tommy had to be rescued from the law. They both hoped Tommy would eventually grow out of his belligerence. Being around Danny didn't help since it seemed Tommy's whole goal in life was to do something so big and important that Danny would be impressed. Roberto thought this was a prescription for disaster.

Both Roberto and Appolina worried most about Danny. For some reason, Maria had a blind eye when it came to her favorite child. Danny was very smart and cunning. It was hard to explain, but at times he seemed ruthless. He thought everyone around him was inferior to him and no matter what the issue, he was always right. As a child, Danny always put forward an angelic face, even though he was invariably the instigator of some bad antics. He often blamed his brothers for things he planned, but then Appolina saw him convince Frank and Tommy that he was only thinking of them and would help them deal with the consequences. The two brothers always fell for his charm. Danny was smart in school but used his good grades to cajole his mother into giving him more freedom. He always had a quick story for where he had been and what he was doing but Appolina didn't believe it. She saw Danny as a bully who got what he wanted and avoided trouble by bribes or threats. She had seen this behavior before in Italy in her brother, Edwardo. He had also been a master manipulator and controlled his mother, father and brothers. In their family only Maria and Appolina saw through Edwardo when they were growing up. Edwardo was the prime reason the girls ran away from the family. Appolina hoped she and Maria were not reliving a smarter, handsomer American version of Edwardo's character, but she worried that it was happening.

Appolina prayed that Danny would straighten up and stop living a phantom life of deceit, but she didn't hold much hope. As long as Maria fell for his alibis, it was a lost cause. Danny could get his brothers to do whatever he wanted. He lived as he liked and told his mother whatever she wanted to hear. Appolina knew he was fooling around with Nora before they were married because she heard him bragging to his brothers about the sex. She found cigars and booze stashed between his clothing in his drawers when she cleaned his room. Later the bottles of booze and the cigars were gone. Either Danny was drinking and smoking a lot or he was using the liquor and cigars as bribes to get something he wanted. Over the years she saw Danny dupe his parents about what was really going on with his life and with his brothers. Appolina begged Roberto to talk to Danny.

"Maybe if you described how bad my brother Edwardo was and you know the trouble Danny could fall into he would listen to you," she implored.

Roberto was reluctant to get involved. He saw trouble coming but didn't want to bring up Edwardo in any discussions. As far as Roberto was concerned, Danny was determining his own life and nothing he would say would stop him. Roberto understood Danny would push back on any lecture Uncle Roberto might deliver. Danny liked his life and was getting away with anything he did. Appolina might see trouble coming, but Roberto did not think confronting Danny would help. He reminded Appolina that people in their little Italian village had confronted Edwardo, to no avail. Edwardo acted as badly, if not worse, after someone called him out. They would have to hope that Danny straightened out. In the meantime, Roberto and Appolina were helpless to step in and change anything. The Russo children were not theirs and other than a comment every now and then there was not much they could say. After all, Vito and Maria were their family and they couldn't risk alienating them over unknown suspicions.

The first big problem with Danny came to light when Nora Gambino's parents showed up at the house. Appolina tried to comfort Maria when they learned Danny knocked up Nora. It was a cruel blow for her sister and she felt terrible. She hoped that the hastily arranged marriage and the new baby would finally set Danny straight. She and Roberto were happy Danny was doing so well in his job and hoped being married would settle him down. But, that never happened. Within weeks of the wedding, Danny announced he had to have a place in Hartford to stay when his work schedule demanded more time. Because Appolina and Roberto had no room in their house to keep him he quickly found a small apartment he could use when he worked late and couldn't get back to Wallingford. Appolina immediately saw this as a way for Danny to neglect his wife and child. Who in the family would really know how many hours Danny spent at Penn Manufacturing and how many hours he spent out on the town in Hartford? Appolina thought it was all very convenient for Danny.

Then the tragedy of the gas accident happened. When the phone rang telling Roberto and Appolina that Nora and Henry were dead they were stunned. They sat together in their small living room and hugged each other. A death of a wife and baby, it seemed unimaginable. They both began to think of all the warning signs they had seen in Danny's treatment of his family. Roberto slowly raised his head.

"Do you believe it?" he whispered to Appolina.

Appolina's heart sank. She knew exactly what Roberto was suggesting. She had just thought it herself. She shook her head slowly, "No."

"What can we do or say?"

Appolina began to cry. Through her tears she wailed,

"We cannot say anything. It is not our place. He is my sister's son. The police will find out the truth. If we say anything we will lose our family. I cannot bear to lose Nora, the baby and my sister all at once."

She began to sob uncontrollably. Through choking tears she continued,

"Maria saved my life when we left Italy. She made it

possible for you and me to be together. It will kill her if we even suggest that Danny had a hand in this. Please, Roberto, please do this for me. Do not say anything."

Roberto agreed, but they both knew it would be hard to keep silent. Danny's treatment of his wife and child had been horrible. He neglected them and probably lived a separate life in Hartford as if they didn't exist. Now that they did not exist, Appolina had proof that Danny was not exactly the grieving husband and father that most people would expect a few weeks after burying a family. Not saying anything was all she and Roberto could do, but deep down, Appolina knew Danny was living a life that was far from good.

Appolina had to tell Roberto what she saw today in the department store in Hartford. It was so soon after the funeral and Danny and the pretty girl were so cozy, she couldn't believe the girl was someone he just met. And, in a way, if it was someone he had just met, that was worse. Did he have no shame? Wasn't he mourning the death of his wife and child in any way? Why not? She remembered the conversation with Roberto right after they heard about the gas accident. Maybe Danny hadn't been so shaken at the funeral. Maybe it had all been an act. She wasn't ready to say he had killed Nora and the child, but she was ready to think that he wasn't sorry they were gone. How could he be sorry if he was in a store less than one month later nuzzling another woman and buying her gloves. He called this woman "his girl"! Appolina walked into the bedroom and laid down on the bed. She had her hand over her eyes and she was shaking. There was so much here that was wrong. What could she and Roberto do? What could her sister do? There were no good answers.

# March 25, 1947 – DEE

D ee left work and headed for her meeting with Danny. She missed him since she last saw him on Saturday. They were a couple and she loved telling her family, her friends, and anyone she met that they were dating. In the last few months he had taken her to wonderful places. They both enjoyed gambling and went to the horse races all the time. She always took ten dollars with her and played until she either lost it all or won some money. She was careful not to ask Danny what he bet on any race because she thought it was a lot more than she would ever wager and she didn't want to seem like a piker. She guessed when he won because she suspected that where they went for dinner was always fancier when he won than when he lost. They also attended dances at the Knights of Columbus Hall and began to make some friends. Danny seemed happy to have her at his side. He would come to the apartment and discuss what she would wear out that evening and then she would slip into the bathroom and dress and show him how she looked. He had lots of opinions on what she wore. He even took her shopping a few times to buy her nice things like gloves and dresses but she tried to avoid doing that too often. She was afraid it would look like she was just using him for his higher salary. She didn't want her family to think she liked him for his money.

One issue was becoming a problem. Danny was pushing her to have sex. They were doing everything but sex now, and she admitted she was liking it, but to have intercourse was beyond her. She tried to explain to him that she was brought up to wait until she was married to go all the way, but he wasn't buying it. At first she thought they could talk about it, but instead of a discussion, it usually led to an argument. Danny said there were ways he could be sure she wouldn't get pregnant. In fact, he didn't want her to get pregnant, but she was driving him crazy with her holding out. Sometimes he became so angry when she pushed him away that he would start shouting at her and accusing her of being a tease. Once he even jumped out of the bed and began to punch the wall next to the headboard. She was actually frightened that he might punch her, but he settled down and got dressed and left her apartment. She wasn't sure she would hear from him again but he called her the next day and acted as though nothing had happened. She let it go. She liked Danny very much and she didn't want to lose him. She absolutely didn't want to have to start dating someone new again.

Dee thought one night he might force her to let him have sex with her. She tried to squirm away from him, but instead of pressing her further, he stopped. She was glad because if he had forced her she would have thrown him out. There was a part of Danny that was tough and violent. The way he reacted was strange to Dee. Dee's family could argue with each other for hours but they never came to any physical abuse to each other. Dee wondered if growing up with boys in a family, like Danny, had meant there was more physical violence, maybe they were used to wrestling or punching each other.

She tried to understand how it would be different than the way she and her sisters treated each other when they fought. Maybe this was normal behavior among men and she didn't understand it because she never saw it in her upbringing. Danny's strength was in some ways an allure to Dee, but in other ways it scared her. She thought she was being silly to worry because whenever she pushed back hard, Danny did stop.

Tonight they planned to get a quick hamburger and see a movie. Danny had been busy at work the last few days and Dee spent her free nights cleaning her apartment and organizing her closet. She was ready for some Danny cuddling, which he did where ever they were. At first it bothered her because he did it so freely in public but after a while she began to like it. She thought it was nice that a guy felt this way about her. Her parents taught the girls not to show any public displays of affection. It was considered inappropriate in her family. As Dee let Danny hold her hand, kiss her cheek or put his arm around her in public she realized maybe her parents were a little too harsh on the subject of public affection. After all, who did it hurt to have Danny want to touch her whenever he could. Dee was feeling the difference in the attitudes of a cold family and a hot lover. She admitted to herself she liked the hot lover Danny was.

Dee took Danny to meet Mary and George. They thought he was smart and interesting. George was impressed with how much Danny knew about machine work. Dee asked Mary if she thought Danny was handsome.

Mary said, "Yes, in a very Italian way."

Dee realized this was Mary's way of saying Danny was

dark. Mary liked light skinned and blond men, like George, her husband. Dee decided not to ask Mary about Danny's looks again. Dee bragged to Mary and George about how successful Danny was at Penn Manufacturing. She knew that anything she told them would make its way back to her parents in Scranton. She wondered when she could ask Danny to go to Scranton with her. He hadn't mentioned meeting his parents yet and she thought it would be best to wait for him to say it before she brought "meeting the parents" up. Dee was thinking that life with Danny might be OK. He was interesting and they agreed on most subjects. Dee sometimes worried that he spent money too freely and cared too much about nice clothes and fancy cars, but he was being paid well and he deserved to enjoy his income. As long as she didn't think he was overextending himself, she thought it would be all right. She learned not to be shocked when he bought a new suit or a few new ties, even though the clothes he had were still perfectly good. Dee's upbringing when it came to money was so tightly controlled that Danny's free spending bothered her. She kept telling herself that the way she was raised did not mean Danny had to act the same way. He was so successful at work and talked about wanting to be even more successful that she began to believe it didn't matter if they had totally different ideas about money and how it was used.

The only real fight they had had since they met was over the sex issue. Dee thought that letting him touch her, kiss her, fondle her breasts and rub against her would placate him, but it wasn't working. If they got very serious and if, she was almost scared to say it, he asked her to marry him, she knew the sex issue would go away. She wouldn't give in on the waiting for the wedding night, but as soon as that was done, the only problem they seemed to have would disappear. She never considered whether or not she would like sex with Danny. But since she had never experienced intercourse, it was hard for her to imagine if she would or would not like it when they were married.

Now she just wanted to get to the burger joint and see him.

# March 26, 1947 – DANNY

Danny was headed to work, thinking about last night with Dee. They got a quick burger and saw a movie. He couldn't tell you what the film was about, he was so busy fantasizing about Dee's body and fucking her. Having sex with Dee had become an obsession. In the past three months he treated her as well as any man could treat a woman. He took her to dinner, dances, movies and the race track. They were having a great time. Each evening she responded to his caresses and his kisses, but when he really wanted to get her naked she absolutely shut down. He was living with a constant hard on and it was not fun. Sometimes it made him so angry he thought about just forcing her. She might succumb if he got her naked and licked her pussy before sticking his dick in her but he couldn't be sure she wouldn't scream and press charges. With Nora's death just a few months before he was careful not to be involved with any police. He knew this was a very bad time for him to be involved in any charges especially with a woman. He didn't need the noise or problems that would come with an accusation. And even though Dee might hesitate to press charges, he worried that part of her was so tied up in waiting for the wedding night for sex because she was so Catholic she would feel compelled to do something to save her image. He wished that he could just walk away, but Danny Russo didn't give up on something he wanted. He always got what he wanted. It was not in his nature to fail. He wanted Dee and he was going to get her. And, he supposed that more than anything he didn't want anyone else to have her.

Dee introduced Danny to her sister and her husband, Mary and George Vitas. They were nice people. George had a great sense of humor and Mary, although pretty uptight, after a drink or two, could get rowdy. They spent evenings playing cards together when the kids were asleep. Danny liked their home and their kids were nice enough. They had a girl, Dorothy, and two boys, Andy and Joey. The youngest boy, Joey, was beautiful. He had white blond hair and incredible blue eyes. Danny thought that at some point in his life it would be cool to have a son like Joey, but that could wait awhile. His last attempt at fatherhood hadn't been very interesting, so knowing Joey through Dee's family was just fine for him now. It was fun to play around with the three year old, throwing him in the air and catching him, letting Joey jump on him and hug him. The best part was when Danny was tired of playing with the kid he just came up with a reason to leave the house. It was the perfect way to enjoy a child.

Work was going well and Danny was thinking he could be seeing another promotion soon. He was wondering what he would do with the extra money. Maybe he could buy a better car, or maybe he could take Dee on a vacation to Florida. Except, what was the point of going on a vacation if she wasn't going to put out for him. He would be better

off going to Florida and finding a few hookers while he was
there enjoying the sunshine. How to get Dee to let him have
sex with her was the biggest issue he had. There had to
be a way to make a nice Catholic girl give up her virginity.
He just had to figure it out. Why would a girl like Dee finally
give in? He pulled into the Penn parking lot and waved at
a coworker and his wife who both worked for the company.
They were chatting and smiling as they walked into the
building. He had seen them together a few times and they
always looked happy. They probably also had a great sex
life. Maybe his last marriage left such a bitter taste for him
because he never really liked being with Nora. Even when
they were having sex it was all about getting the sex and
saying goodbye. They never did anything together and they
certainly never did anything with each other after the wedding. Danny couldn't remember a single time that he and
Nora discussed something that led to their smiling at each
other. Sitting in his car he looked again at the couple and
realized what he had to do. He had to marry Dee. Unlike
Nora, Dee and Danny had lots to say to each other. They
both enjoyed discussing and comparing their work. They
had a great time going out to dinner and playing the ponies. Danny and Dee often spent time talking about the
future and what it would be like to own a home and have
nice things. They enjoyed spending time with George and
Mary and Danny had some great laughs playing with the
Vitas kids. When Danny thought about avoiding marriage
he realized that what was wrong with marriage was that
Danny had married the wrong woman when he got hitched
to Nora. Of course, he never planned to be with Nora, so

it followed that it wasn't a good match. It was just a trap that Nora sprang on him when he was a lot younger and stupider. Danny realized he was avoiding marriage because of Nora, rather than looking for marriage with someone he wanted to be with and especially wanted to screw, like Dee.

In an instant, Danny decided to ask Dee to marry him. He was sure she would say yes, but could he go through with it? This was going to be more complicated than a normal proposal. Danny would have to tell Dee he had been married before. He was worried she would find out and cancel the wedding if he hid his marriage to Nora from her. He would have to deal with his mother and father who would wonder at how fast he had found someone else. Then there was his aunt, Appolina, who he knew didn't always buy his act. He would have to make sure she was convinced that Dee was the real thing. He wasn't too worried about that since Dee always came off as level headed and mature. He thought his parents and his aunt and uncle would be impressed by her. In fact, Dee would make getting his family's approval easier than not. She was lovely, from a solid family with a solid job. He thought they would see why he was attracted to her and why he was not exactly thrilled with his marriage to Nora.

Most importantly, he would have to convince Dee that he needed his own time away from time to time. After all, he couldn't imagine a life time with only one woman. He wanted Dee but he was realistic enough to know Dee wouldn't satisfy him forever. There would always be younger beautiful women who he could meet. And he didn't envision passing up great opportunities with other women just because he was married. He needed Dee to understand from the beginning that he would be away from time to time for work. Nora had accepted the arrangement, now if he could get Dee to play along the same set up would work just fine for him. He would talk to Dee this weekend. He should get her some flowers and a ring. In fact, the new promotion would help with the cost of the ring. It had to be big enough to impress Dee but not so big that she would start scolding him because he spent too much money. Her constant harping on saving money was getting tiring. He had to have her stop talking about how she saved so much and so should he. But, none of that mattered if he could only finally get her in bed. He wanted Dee so much he could taste it. It was time.

Three weeks later, Danny was sitting in his parents' living room explaining his decision to marry Dee. His aunt and uncle were there. Maria wanted to know about Dee and her family. Danny said he met them recently and they were good people. Maria asked him why it had to be so soon after Nora and Henry died. Danny put on his most mournful face and looked directly at his mother,

"I'm lonely. I never thought I could be so lost. The accident took away part of my life. I was living to work and not doing much else. Meeting Dee changed all that. She is so level headed and hard working. She made me whole again. She makes me want to live."

His mother reached out and patted his hand. She thought it was very soon, but he was only 31 and it was hard to imagine that a young man could wait forever before wanting his life to go forward. Appolina cleared her throat,

"Danny, when did you meet Dee?"

He hesitated a second and seemed to be thinking back. "I guess I met her in February. Yes, around mid February when a friend from work set us up. I didn't want to go because it was still so close to Nora's passing, but Dee was so nice and interested in me. I was immediately taken with her."

Appolina nodded and glanced to Roberto. He raised his eyebrows and she knew he understood. Danny was lying. Nothing had changed.

# June 15, 1948 – GEORGE

Dorothy and Andy were squealing with laughter. The kids loved splashing in the waves and digging in the sand. George Vitas thought hearing his children laugh was the greatest sound in the world. He and Mary had taken the children to a small lake in southern Massachusetts where Danny and Dee were building a cottage as a second home. They still lived and worked in Hartford, but Danny was doing so well they decided to get a weekend place. Actually, Danny decided to get a weekend place and Dee, as always, went along with his idea. George and Mary loved the chance to take the kids away from the city and give the older kids, Dorothy and Andy swimming lessons. It was a beautiful day and George loved being in the water with the kids. Mary sat on a folding chair on the small beach holding Joey, the baby.

The Vitas' had come to the lake a number of times to help Danny with his cottage. It was a simple structure and Danny was very good with any type of building project. He and George had already framed the structure and installed the windows. They were ready to start the drywalling which George promised to help with right after lunch. By then the kids would be tired and the baby would be napping so the men could get to work on the dry wall and Dee and Mary would clean up from lunch and get dinner ready. Danny had rigged up a lean-to tent next to the cottage that they used for shelter when they went to the lake.

Helping Danny was easy because George was a good worker and Danny was easy to work with. He was smart about the supplies, tools and time different jobs would take. Danny and Dee had been married about two years. Dorothy had been a flower girl in their wedding. She said she felt like a princess the day of the wedding with her beautiful long dress and flowers. Since the wedding Danny had come and gone from the Vitas house in Hartford at will. He would often show up as George was fixing a faucet or a stuck door and pitch right in to help. For about three months Mary complained that she needed a cabinet in the kitchen to hold her pots and pans and give her some counter space. One day Danny arrived with wood, supplies and a counter top and spent the day building Mary a kitchen cabinet. She was ecstatic when he was done.

George could not thank him enough for the cabinet and his help. Danny seemed to have endless energy and was amazingly talented when it came to everyday fix it and build it chores. George felt he owed Danny help at the lake since Danny always helped them without being asked.

The problem was that it was not always smooth sailing with Danny. More than once Dee had called Mary in tears over some terrible fight Danny and she had. Once Mary was so worried about Dee's crying on the phone that Mary had George go over to Dee and Danny's apartment and break up the fight. George hated that day because he saw a side to Danny that he couldn't believe. Danny was livid when George got to the apartment. The door was unlocked so he let himself

in. Danny had backed Dee against a wall and was screaming in her face. The fight was about some money issue, but
the wild look in Danny's eyes was what was truly frightening.
George managed to get between the two of them so Dee
could slip away and then Danny turned his fury on George.
George was smaller than Danny, but very strong. He was not
going to put up with this treatment.

"Calm down Danny. You have no right to scare Dee, and
you better not think about threatening me."

Danny's eyes only got wilder,

"You stupid jerk, who asked you to butt in here. I am going to kill her. She has everything in the world and just keeps
complaining. I've had it with her bull."

Danny tried to push George away, but George pushed
back on Danny.

"Well, if you're going to kill her you're going to kill me
first. I have no idea what this fight is about, but you have no
right to scare your wife like this. Stop it or we're calling the
police."

Mentioning the police seemed to have an impact on
Danny. He suddenly looked down. He lowered his arms. And
took a step back. He looked at Dee like he did want to kill her
and then turned and walked to the door. He hesitated at the
door and turned back to the table along the wall and picked
up his car keys. He walked slowly out of the apartment. Dee
and George just looked at each other. A few moments later,
they heard the Cadillac's tires squeal as Danny pulled out of
the parking space and headed down the street.

"Dee, you should come home with me. I don't want you
here alone when he comes back."

Dee shook her head.

"No, I know what he'll do. He won't come home until to-morrow and he'll act like nothing happened. I'm not sure why he went so crazy. It happened so quickly. I asked him where he got the money for some stuff he brought home and he just lost it. He started screaming at me and tore apart the bedroom. That's when I called Mary. It wasn't even that much money, but it was like he was ready to explode about any-thing. Maybe he had some trouble at work." Dee began to cry softly, "I am so sorry you had to come here."

George gave her a hug.

"No, I'm glad I came. He was pretty out of control. But, I am still worried about you being here alone."

Dee said she would be fine and just wanted to go lie down. She was sure she wouldn't see Danny until the next day. She showed George out the door and he heard her click the bolt lock after he left. George was happy about that, at least Danny wouldn't be able to get in if he did return in a foul mood.

For all the good times with Danny, George was always a bit wary of what would come next. He talked with Mary about Dee getting divorced but Mary was adamant that Dee would never do that. They were too Catholic to consider such a dras-tic idea. Dee was not about to give up her religion over one or two fights. George had to accept that Dee and Danny were going to be around for the long haul.

Now they were going to put up dry wall. The ladders were in place and the hammers and nails were ready to go. George and Danny spent a good afternoon making great progress on the drywall installation. The men discussed the

Red Sox season and the next time they would be able to get away and play the ponies. About six o'clock the kids were hungry and Dee and Mary put out the salad and meat for dinner. When they finished George piled everyone into the car for the hour trip home. The kids were all asleep before they got to the house so Mary and he took turns carrying them up to their bedrooms.

# June 21, 1950 - MARY

M ary ran to the phone in the hallway. How could she be so stupid. Just a few minutes before she had walked into the house to change the laundry. By the time she returned to the front yard Joey was gone. She screamed for the other children and Dorothy and Andy came running. She pulled them close and quickly asked them if they knew where Joey was. Both children were frightened of how hard she was holding them. They shook their heads, "No."

"We were playing in the back yard and Joey was out here with you. Is he gone?" Dorothy, at age eight sounded almost like an adult. Mary was frantic.

"I don't know. Andy, search the house and look in the attic and the basement for Joey. And check that the baby is still sleeping in her crib. Call for me as loudly as you can if you find anything. Dorothy, run up the block and down the block and look in all the yards and on the house porches for Joey. If you see him bring him right back here. Don't leave the block, just come right back when you're done. Now go." She pushed them away.

Grabbing the phone she quickly dialed the police. She tried to calm herself to talk intelligently. She was afraid she would start crying and screaming at the same time.

"This is Mrs. Vitas, I live at 30 Madison Ave. in Hartford. I am reporting that my 4 year old son is missing." As she said the words she started to cry.

"Mrs. Vitas, is that correct? The officer tried to hear her through her sobs. "Mrs. Vitas, please try to pull yourself together so we can get the information we need and find your son. Have you looked everywhere in the house and around the yard where he might be?"

"Yes", she screamed.

"Ok. Your address is 30 Madison Avenue in Hartford, correct? Can you describe the child to me? Height, weight, color of hair, color of eyes and what he is wearing? Where was the last place you saw him and when was that?"

The questions seemed to take forever.

"Please, send someone to help. He's been gone for almost 30 minutes."

"Yes, Mrs. Vitas, we're dispatching patrol cars now. Please stay on the line. I have a few more questions for you." The officer's voice was calming, but Mary was anything but calm.

Somehow Mary got through all the questions just as Andy and Dorothy appeared before her.

"Did you find him?" she eagerly asked looking from face to face.

Both children shook their heads, "no."

Her heart sank. Andy piped up, "But the baby is in the crib sleeping. That's good, right Mom?"

She pulled both children to her as she cradled the phone under her chin. "Yes, that is good. Please go sit in the living room."

"Mrs. Vitas. You have other children? Are they accounted for and safe?" the officer holding on the phone line was trying to get her attention.

"Yes, the other three are fine, but where is Joey?" She thought her head would burst. She was so frightened she couldn't think straight, and she couldn't breathe. She began to get light headed. She was panicked she would faint and scare the other children. Who would take care of the baby when she woke up from her nap? Suddenly she heard sirens and realized there were police cars in front of the house. She slammed down the phone and ran to the front door.

"Have you found him," she practically jumped the officer walking towards her front door.

"Now Mam, please calm down. I know this is very frightening, but most young children reported missing show up within a few hours. They usually wander to another yard, get confused about where they are and get picked up by a friendly neighbor who spends some time giving them milk and cookies and trying to figure out where they live. My officers will start going from house to house to see if we can locate your boy. You said you were in the house and he was alone in the front yard. How long do you think he was alone?"

Mary tried to think back on how long she spent moving the clothes from the washer to the large basket she used to carry the clean pieces to the backyard where she could hang them on the drying line George put up for her. It couldn't have been more than five minutes, maybe 10 at the most. Then she would have picked up Joey and moved him to the back yard with her as she started to hang the laundry. The officer said that was good. Joey couldn't wander very far in ten minutes so she should try to relax and take care of the other children while the police did a sweep of the neighborhood. He asked her for a recent picture and she ran into the house and pulled one out of the kitchen drawer. The picture was taken when they brought the new baby home. Joey stood proudly next to Mary who held the baby. Joey looked like he was happy to be the older brother. Mary caught her breath when she looked at it. She walked back outside and showed the picture to the policeman. He thanked her and told her to go back in the house.

She appreciated how calm and sure the cop was they would find Joey, but there was a nagging thought in her head that Joey had never wandered out of the yard before. What would make him do this today? She went back into the house and considered calling George at work but getting a call that their son was gone would make her husband frantic. She imagined him racing home in a panic. If Joey reappeared in a few minutes she would feel silly dragging George from his factory job in such a state. She thought she would wait. She went and checked on the new baby who was still sleeping and then sat down with Dorothy and Andy on the living room couch.

"Will Joey be all right?" Andy looked scared as he asked.

She answered, "Yes, the officers say they think they will find him quickly. I think we should say a prayer to Jesus to be sure Joey is safe wherever he is and that he comes home soon."

The children folded their hands and bowed their heads. She made up a small prayer about Jesus and his Mother loving babies and taking care of Joey with their love. She ended with a whispered "Amen." The three of them settled back on the couch and stared ahead. Mary wasn't sure what was the best thing to do. She couldn't leave her children and the baby alone while she ran around the neighborhood. And she was only one person while the cops had about five officers walking the street. They were obviously going to cover much more territory than she could alone. She looked at the clock on the mantle and made a deal with herself. She would sit quietly for twenty minutes then she would go outside and see if the policeman had any news. If he did not, she would call George at work and ask him to come home. She would say she was feeling lousy so he wouldn't panic and that she needed to go to the doctor. He would come home quickly, but he would not be frantic. She knew she didn't need her husband in a car accident racing home on top of having her child missing.

The clock ticked slowly forward. The children didn't move. Mary was not sure any of them were breathing. As the twenty minute mark passed she stood up. It had been more than an hour, almost two hours, since she first discovered Joey was gone. She had to do something.

"Kids will you play quietly in the house and let me know if the baby wakes up? I'll be in the yard speaking with the police officer." They nodded yes and she turned and walked out the front door.

The police were beginning to gather in front of the house. When she saw the look on the officer's face she knew it was not good news.

"Sorry, Mam, but we're coming up short on the sweep of the street. We're going to put out an all points bulletin and distribute an enlarged picture of your boy. Are you sure that the description you gave of his clothes is correct? This looks like this will have to be elevated to kidnapping."

Mary started to collapse, the officer caught her under her elbows and held her up.

She swayed on her feet and doubled over again. The officer continued to hold her up.

"Would you like to go into the house and get some water?" he asked.

She didn't think she could make it back into the house to call George. How could she ever use the word "kidnapping" to her husband. How could she ever face her husband? How could she go on living?

Just then a large, Cadillac sedan drove up to the house. Mary barely raised her head as the driver leaned over and opened the passenger door. Joey sprang out, dressed in cowboy chaps and a cowboy hat with a gun belt and six shooter slung around his waist.

"Mommy, mommy, Uncle Danny took me to ride a pony and he got me cowboy clothes to take the picture. Uncle Danny said I was the best cowboy ever!"

Mary ran to Joey and scooped him up in her arms. She was crying and hugging and kissing him all at once. Danny got out of the driver's seat and walked up to the group standing before the police cars. Joey was excited about his great outing and his new clothes. He kept saying the pony was really big and Uncle Danny let him sit on the pony by himself. Joey was ecstatic. Mary glared at Danny. She carefully put Joey down and told him to go into the house and show his new things to his brother and sister. He ran happily through the front door.

Mary turned on Danny and lunged at him. She tried to gouge out his eyes, she screamed every profanity she knew. She wanted to kill him. He grabbed her wrists and stopped her from pummeling his chest. He couldn't believe how wild her eyes were. She looked demented, and she continued to flail at him. He had trouble controlling her.

"Jesus, Mary, I only had the kid for a few hours. It wasn't for days. I saw a guy with a pony taking pictures of children riding the horse. I thought it would be fun to get Joey dressed and take a picture of him as a real cowboy. Was that such a horrible idea?"

Mary looked up at Danny with the fury of God in her eyes. The officer saw it and stepped between them worried Mary might actually harm Danny, and from her point of view, he couldn't blame her.

"Listen, Mister, well, whoever you are. You just scared the livin' daylights out of this woman. We were about to lodge a kidnapping complaint. You're lucky you got here before we did. No one looks kindly on people who snatch children, for any reason, cowboy outfits with ponies or not. You better start apologizing and Mrs. Vitas." The officer turned to Mary, "If you want to swear out a complaint against this man, be my guest. He should never have done what he did."

Mary looked at Danny and looked at the officer. She was so angry she was shaking. She turned to Danny, "Get away from my house and stay away from my children. You are a maniac and are not welcome here."

Danny was shocked,

"Come on, Mary, it was all in good fun. You know I would never hurt your kids. Hell, you're Dee's family. What's the big deal that I took Joey without telling you? I knew we would be back soon. Give it a break, there's no reason to react like this." Danny was starting to talk louder and louder as though he could get everyone to agree with him if he had the most forceful voice. "Christ, it was only for an hour or so, you're making it seem as though he was lost or taken. What a typical female overreaction. Jesus."

The officer raised his eyebrows and stepped closer to Danny.

"Now, just a minute, mister. You scared the hell out of this woman and she has every right to be angry and press charges. If I were you I'd be begging her forgiveness and saying you will do anything for her."

Danny sneered at the cop and took a step back. He didn't want to take this guy on with the other cops standing by, but if he could have he would have. He hated when someone treated him like he'd done something wrong. He looked down and tried to resist throwing a punch at the officer. He slowly turned to Mary as if to see if she was going to go along with him or the policeman.

Mary wasn't sure she could speak. Her head was splitting and she thought she had lost a few years of her life. She needed to sit quietly with her children and breath normally. She certainly wanted the circus in front of her home to go away. She looked at the officer and swallowed the horrible taste in her mouth.

"Thank you for your time, sir. I am so sorry we caused this ruckus. It won't happen again."

The officer looked at her and at Danny, "How about a complaint against this man. He's admitted he took the child without telling you. Do you want to press charges?"

Mary thought of Dee and their parents. She thought of the trouble with lawyers and the cost. She wondered what George would do. Suddenly, Dorothy, Andy and Joey all burst out the front door and ran to Danny.

"Uncle Danny, Uncle Danny, can you take us for Ice Cream?" they chanted. Danny glanced at Mary and down at the children. He cleared his throat and said,

"Not today kids. I have to get back to some work at my office. We'll do it the next time I'm around." Each of the children was holding onto him. The boys were on his legs and Dorothy was holding his arm.

Mary looked at the cop. She realized she couldn't bring this problem on her family. She was furious at Danny but there was no doubt he was part of the family and most of the time he was very good with the children. "No Officer, I won't be pressing charges. Thanks again."

She turned and called the children to follow her. They walked into the house together. Dorothy led the way and held the door open for Andy and Joey. Mary nodded for Dorothy to follow the boys inside and slowly closed the door. Mary heard the squad cars leaving and Danny's car start. The Cadillac drove off with a squeal of tires. Mary hated him and wanted him gone. She felt Andy take her hand and shake her. She looked down at him.

"Mommy why didn't Uncle Danny take all of us to have our pictures with the pony?"

Mary thought about that for a minute. It would be best not to scare the children and explain what Danny had done. She decided to make it as small an issue as she could with the kids. She said softly,

"I think it was because he was worried the man with the pony would leave quickly and he wouldn't get any pictures. If you were all in the front yard he might have taken all of you." Andy thought about that for a moment and seemed to accept that they were just not in the right place to be included. Mary heard a noise from the second floor. She let go of Andy's hand and said, "I hear the baby crying. Please stay in the house and play until dinner time. We've had enough excitement for one day around here."

Dorothy, Andy and Joey went off to the kitchen to play with their blocks on the floor and she climbed the stairs to get the baby. She was still very angry. This would not go away quickly.

# June 21, 1950 – DEE

D ee sat in the red velvet chair in Danny and her apartment's living room. The chair matched the large, red velvet couch on the opposite side of the room which sat on the red, yellow and blue oriental rug Danny made them buy. The lamps, the tables and the pictures on the walls, indeed, the entire room, had been decorated by Danny and some woman he met at the furniture store. Dee went along because Danny demanded she be there. Dee knew Danny wanted to say they picked out the furniture together, but Dee was barely involved. The whole thing was too expensive for her. Why did they need to spend so much money on furniture not many people would see or use? Dee knew they needed some furniture when they were married and moved to the larger apartment on Ward Street in Hartford. She even believed Danny when he said they could afford it. What she couldn't do was enjoy it. It was only for show. They spent most of their time in the kitchen or small sitting area immediately inside the front door where the TV was set up. This room was off to the side of the apartment. To Dee it was expensive and only more space she needed to clean. Dee didn't even want to think about the bedroom. That room had become her prison and the less time she was there, the better.

Dee was trying to understand the call she just had from

George Vitas, her brother in law. George calling to talk to her wasn't usual. Dee almost always heard from Mary who organized what they would be doing together and when. Mary always handed out the assignments for large family dinners and what everyone was supposed to make and bring. Mary also set the calendar for when they played cards and when they went to Scranton to visit their parents. If Mary needed to have the children watched, she always called Dee and they talked about the drop off and pick up times. But today George called. Dee was not happy about the conversation. And, no surprise, the issue was Danny.

Since they were married three years ago, Danny had angered George and Mary a few times. He had angered Dee countless times. The issues almost always centered on Danny losing his temper and calling George, Mary or Dee idiots or dumb bells. Danny was always right and everyone else was stupid. Dee was used to it because Danny's abuse to her started within a week of the wedding. Dee never told anyone, including Mary, how Danny acted when they were alone. George and Mary didn't like it when Danny erupted, but usually got over it in a day or two. When they had a fight Danny always made up to George and Mary by doing something nice for them. He once showed up at their house and built them a kitchen cabinet which he knew Mary wanted and he knew George didn't know how to do. Danny was good with his hands and loved doing woodwork. Everyone saw it was Danny's way of saying he was sorry. George was appreciative and Mary was ecstatic she finally got the kitchen cabinet she needed which meant Danny was back in their good graces quickly. Another time Danny showed up at George and Mary's house the day after he had a screaming match with George. Danny took the older kids, Dorothy and Andy for ice cream at the local dairy, giving Mary a few hours break from the daily chores rearing three, and since the recent birth of the baby, four children. Dee watched Danny maneuver around George and Mary and realized Danny was careful around George. How Danny acted around her was much worse than how he acted around the Vitas. Dee thought Danny knew George was a very strong person and Danny had to be careful around him. Dee was glad George had some sway over Danny because a few times in the last three years Danny scared her. Dee thought George would protect her from Danny if she needed it.

Unfortunately, Danny figured out within a week of the wedding that he could treat Dee anyway he wanted. Dee admitted to herself that the problem was she didn't know what was expected of a wife, specifically what was expected for sex when you were married. She was so confused. How was she supposed to know what to do? She couldn't figure out how to find out what she should be doing because it appalled her to think anyone would discuss such things. Her mother and father never made a reference of any kind to sex when she was growing up in Scranton and her sisters were both married and having babies, but never breathed a word about what went on in the bedroom. Dee thought talking about such things might even be a mortal sin. In the beginning she tried to laugh off the silly things Danny wanted, only to learn they were no laughing matter to him. She learned quickly to be quiet and follow his instructions. When he told her to undress slowly in front of him and dance to some sultry music he put on the Victrola, she now did it without a protest. When he said he wanted to fuck her multiple times in a night, she laid back and tried to think of other things. When he sucked her breasts and made her sit on his penis she complied. When he made her splay her legs so he could lick her while making her suck his penis she wanted to vomit, but she learned to push down the urge. As he told her over and over again,

"I waited a long time for this baby and I'm going to make up for the wait. You are going to make me happy like I have never been happy before."

Danny never mentioned Dee's happiness.

In the last year Danny was promoted at Penn Manufacturing again. He told Dee he was on target to be the youngest Vice President in the history of the company. He was thinking of buying yet another new car. He was looking at the new Cadillacs that had just come out. Dee asked if his new promotion changed his hours or what he had to do at work. He looked at her for a long time and drew a long breath,

"I'm glad you brought that up because if I do make VP soon it will change some things and I may be away even more. I will be totally at the beck and call of the company. Not only will I have to stay late whenever something important is going on, I'll also have to travel more. I don't know how much, but I've seen some of the other VPs and they're on the road a lot. You'll have to get used to me being gone more and more. Of course, I'll be home whenever I can, but just know that at any moment, I might have to call you and change my plans. It's all part of the package. This nice apartment, great furniture, nice car and everything we have is dependent on how I do in the next few years. You understand? Who knows, baby, maybe in a few years we can think of upgrading from the lake cottage to a larger second place, somewhere nice like down at the beach so we can spend more time off away from the city."

Dee nodded yes. She even smiled and said she was happy for his success. She would do whatever she needed to do. Mostly she was glad to hear she might have some time by herself where he wouldn't be around to demand her services, particularly at night. She had her job, her family here and in Scranton and she had her friends. Part of her wondered if he was making this up so he could do as he pleased, but this was one fight she wasn't going to start. If he was really going to be away she wasn't so sad. She had married Danny with her eyes wide open and now she had to live with her decision. If he made it easier for her to get through each day by leaving her alone, that was OK.

Now she was sitting in the dumb living room she hardly ever walked into waiting for Danny to come home so she could discuss George's call. She didn't know where Danny was because he no longer bothered to tell her when he was coming home. She wondered why he was driving around Hartford in the middle of the afternoon when he grabbed Joey for the picture on the pony. Why wasn't he at work? She knew he still worked at Penn because he gave her steady money for the house and food. She saw the bills come into the house and he took them away, to be paid. But his taking Joey without telling Mary and having the policemen involved was very bad. George was livid and wanted Danny to either call him or come over to the house to see him. Dee dreaded confronting Danny and couldn't figure out where this would go. She didn't know what she would do if Danny didn't come home. Dee almost never mentioned Danny's absences to her family. But if he didn't appear soon she would have to tell George she couldn't find Danny. Where that would lead she didn't know. So far she had kept from her family and friends that Danny was often gone and she didn't know where he went. She could say he was needed at work, but that wouldn't work with Danny's antics with Joey while he was riding around in the middle of the day. Dee wished that he would just come home. She could tell him to call George and then get ready for the explosion. She knew Danny would not like being yelled at and she could hardly disagree with George when the cops were suggesting they charge Danny with a crime.

Dee heard Danny's key in the lock. He walked into the apartment and called her name. She responded that she was in the living room. Danny came into the room holding a bouquet of flowers.

"Hi baby. What's up?"

She looked at him and looked down at the carpet. For some reason she had an immediate dislike of the rug. It made her weary.

"I was thinking of going over to Mary and George's house. Do you want to come? I took Joey for a picture today and Mary didn't hear me call out to her that I was taking him. She called the cops. We sorted it all out. I bought these flowers to help her mood. I also went to the police station and left some cigars for the cops. They were nice to help her out until I brought Joey back."

He seemed to be trying out this story on her to see if she would buy it. She thought this was very Danny, always a smooth story to get around what had happened. He was never in the wrong, it was Mary's fault that she didn't hear him. If it wasn't so disgusting it would be funny. She looked at the flowers and at him.

"No, you go. I've already spoken with George. He isn't happy. Good luck."

Danny stood in front of her trying to figure out what she was thinking and how his version of the afternoon went over. Dee continued to stare at the floor. Danny turned and left.

# October 15, 1953 – DANNY

D anny was in a good mood. He thought his promotion to Vice President at Penn Manufacturing was a done deal. It was just a matter of time. Two weeks ago, he convinced the engineering guys to make a small change in the design of a part and it worked. The client and the company were very happy with his innovation. He needed a win because some of his work at Penn lately had led down dead ends. Danny's identity at Penn rested on always coming up with improvements to the Manufacturing process for Penn's customers. When his ideas fell flat he was concerned that he would be seen as a lightweight. If a few of his ideas failed in a row he became desperate. Seven years ago, when he was a new employee at Penn if something didn't work out his defense was to blame others for the bad outcomes, even if they had nothing to do with it. He paid off a few guys who wanted to expose him, but that tactic had backfired on him after some of the guys he paid started to talk and he knew that some of the younger executives were watching him to be sure he took both the blame and credit for what he did. This last week his latest suggestion was a success. He felt he was back in the limelight. As long as he continued to have at least as many good ideas as bad ideas, he thought he would be fine.

The scene in his personal life had also settled down. After

six years of marriage, Dee turned out to be as boring as Nora had been. The difference was that Dee was not as demanding as Nora. Dee had her dumb job at Underwood Company and her family and her endless girlfriends. She almost never depended on Danny to be around or part of her life. He still enjoyed screwing her from time to time. Her body had not lost its allure. But Danny realized having a partner who couldn't or wouldn't be engaged while having sex was a major turn-off, great body or not. His demands for her to have sex were dwindling.

Despite the disappointment of his marriage to Dee, Danny saw the value in having what to the outside world looked like a stable marriage. He always made an effort to show up for Dee's family affairs, like her nieces and nephews birthdays and first communions, and to visit Dee's parents in Scranton with her a few times a year. He also asked Dee to go with him to visit his family in Wallingford. His mother thought Dee was a lovely, hardworking girl, but was obviously disappointed there were no grandchildren. Dee always told his mother, Maria, she wished they could have children, but God had decided otherwise. Maria understood. Her sister, Appolina, had never had children. It was God's will. Danny realized that this arrangement of a marriage of sorts was very easy to continue and gave him lots of freedom. Regardless of how he felt about Dee and their thin marriage, he was happy to have her taking care of the apartment and not getting in his way.

Today Danny was visiting a friend in a bar who was going to get him into a poker game. Danny loved to gamble and was an avid follower of the horses and the fights. He played poker all of his life with his brothers, almost always beating them, so he thought he might be able to make some fast money with a group of guys who played for some meaningful stakes. He parked his Cadillac in a small lot across from the bar and got out. As always, he was dressed in a beautiful grey suit, starched white shirt and striped silk tie. His leather shoes had been shined that morning by the shoeshine guy he used at the corner of his street. He didn't need an overcoat yet because the weather hadn't been very cold this fall. He wondered if he should plan to get a new overcoat for the winter. He decided if his promotion came through soon he would get one.

He walked into the bar and nodded to the bartender.

"Can I have a scotch and soda? And do you know if Ken is around?"

The bartender began to pour the drink and motioned to the back of the bar where a young woman was sitting in a booth by herself.

"Ken couldn't make it but sent his assistant. She asked me to tell her when you got here."

Danny looked at the woman who was partially covered by the shadows from the overhead lights.

"Ok. Thanks."

He walked towards the booth and looked down at her. She was small and blond. Not bad looking but no great beauty. He thought he would get the info and leave quickly. She didn't interest him.

"Hi, I'm Danny Russo. I was planning to meet Ken but the bartender says he couldn't make it."

She looked up from her drink and smiled. It seemed she waited a beat before she started talking.

"Hi, I'm sorry to disappoint you but Ken had a personal emergency and couldn't make it. He wasn't sure how to get a hold of you so he asked me to come here and relay his message."

She seemed to be easy to talk to and indicated with her hand that he should sit down. He put his drink on the table and slid into the booth bench opposite her. There was another awkward pause.

"Oh, I'm sorry, my name if Monica. Monica McNally. I work for Ken at the dispatcher office for the Hartford Trucking Company."

"Hello Monica. Nice to meet you. What's the word from Ken?"

She smiled again at him. She seemed to be sizing him up, looking at his clothes and his hair and his face. He couldn't tell if she was putting on an act, or if she always hesitated before she spoke.

"Ken says that the game is all set up and gave me an envelope with the name, address, and date where you should plan to meet the others." He waited while she rummaged in her pocket book and pulled out a small envelope with his name on the front.

"Thanks so much, Monica. And be sure to thank Ken for me too."

He started to get out of the booth but she pulled on his hand to stop him. He sat back down. Again, the hesitation.

"Do you have to leave right away? You haven't finished your drink?"

He looked at her closely. She wasn't what he was usually attracted to. She was slim, almost skinny and very blond.

She had very blue eyes and very red lips. Her smile was lovely. She was dressed neatly but in nondescript clothes, what Danny would describe as a working girl outfit for someone who worked at a trucking company. She had on a beige sweater and a darker brown pair of slacks. She was carrying a brown and white shoulder pocketbook and had a dull grey coat folded on the seat next to her. Hardly a glamourous get up but then, she did work at a trucking company. He guessed she was about 25.

"No, I don't have to go too soon. And, I would love to finish my drink with an attractive young lady."

He watched her dip her head as though she was blushing and wanted to hide it, but he thought otherwise.

"So, what exactly do you do for Ken? At work, I mean."

She didn't seem to get the joke, so he let it pass. She described how she filled out the dispatch forms which the other ladies in the office reviewed and approved. She didn't actually do much for Ken at the office. He was the big boss and she was very new at the job. It became clear that this outing was about as exciting a thing she had done since she was hired. Danny figured that Ken didn't even know her name until he had this little errand to get done. The older women in the office probably suggested he use Monica because there wasn't much she was doing that they couldn't miss for an afternoon.

By the time they finished their drinks Monica was laughing and talking nonstop. Danny heard about her background in Massachusetts and her time in high school. It seemed that Monica didn't really like high school and couldn't wait to get away from her aunt and uncle who she lived with. She implied she was an orphan and her aunt and uncle already had a family when she was foisted on them. It seemed they hardly noticed when she told them she was leaving to take a job in Connecticut. She said she never intended to go back to see them. That part of her life was over.

Danny wondered why he was bothering with this, but it had been awhile since he's slept with Dee and he was a little horny. Monica was no great beauty but it appeared she was willing. He suggested they head out for a pizza or something and she agreed. The stood up from the booth and headed for the door. Danny noticed that the bartender was talking on the phone and didn't look up when they left.

When they got to the sidewalk in front of the bar Danny asked if she had taken a cab to meet him. Again the hesitation as she looked at him, finally she laughed and said she had taken a bus. She said the women at the office told her to go home after she delivered the message because the bus ride was long and she didn't need to come back that day. Danny thought that was great. No one expected her to be anywhere.

"Ok, we'll take my car." He led her to the parking lot and opened the door of the Cadillac for her. She was clearly impressed with the car. She sank down in the soft leather and put her head against the back of the seat. Danny smiled at her and started the car.

"I know a place we can go that will deliver a pizza as soon as we're hungry. Ok."

She hesitated. "Sure. Why not?" she finally said.

Danny wondered again if this was worth it, but she was young and clearly available so it was convenient. He needed some outlet. Why not, indeed.

Danny took her to a small motel he used from time to time. He parked far away from the office and left her lounging in the front seat as he checked in with the receptionist who knew him from earlier visits. He drove the car around to the back of the property and parked in front of the room he rented. There were no other cars in the parking lot. She looked around and turned to him and smiled. He had a hard time figuring her out. This was a strange mixture of innocence and lust. She seemed so young and fresh, but she was not at all shocked that she was sitting in a stranger's car in a motel parking lot and he was holding a room key.

She got out of the car first and he followed. They went into the room and she dropped her coat and bag. Danny immediately began to kiss her and fondle her breasts. She pushed against him and ground against his body. He was ready to go. In no time he torn off his clothes and then hers. She stood in front of him naked. He backed her to the bed and climbed on top of her. She bit his nipple.

He pushed her back, "Hey, that hurt." Again, she smiled and hesitated before answering.

"I like it when it hurts, don't you?"

Danny was surprised. This was not what he was used to but he could adapt. If she wanted it rough, he could be rough. He slapped her face. She jerked back and turned towards him. Again she smiled and hesitated,

"That's more like it big boy."

Danny totally got into it. She took everything he put to her and she kept smiling. He fucked her for a long time and she scratched and bit him and slapped him back. The orgasm he had was monumental. He was out of breath and sweating as they lay back. He noticed that he had split her lip slightly, probably from one of his slaps. She licked the blood away.

"Baby, you are something." He said between breaths. He waited for the hesitation which came before she answered,

"Yes, I am."

"Are you hungry? Should I order that pizza?"

Again a hesitation.

"No, it can wait. I'd like to know about your job and your life. Are you married? Do you live in Hartford?"

"Well, I would rather not get into the particulars right now. Since we are both lying here naked, maybe that conversation can wait until we're dressed and having a quiet conversation during drinks and a dinner."

She did not seem happy with this response. She got up from the bed and started to pull on her underwear. As she was dressing she started to raise her voice,

"I would like to know NOW. I'm not waiting for a quiet conversation with you!"

He looked at her. Suddenly her voice had changed. There was no hesitation when she spoke and no smile. Her voice was like ice. She continued to dress looking at him accusingly. She pulled on her sweater and slacks and came around to his side of the bed. He looked up at her and started to get off the bed as he said,

"Sorry honey, this is all you get on my info. I think we should get dressed and I'll drop you off where ever you want. I have to get home. I have a big work day planned for tomorrow so I can't stay here long."

She suddenly punched him in the face.

"What the fuck are you doing?" He was stunned.

"I want to know all about you. I've heard of men who pick up girls, beat them up a bit and then drop them. I'm not putting up with that. I want to be able to call you and see you and I want to be driven around in your Cadillac and taken for dinners and movies I want you to pay for what you did to me here."

Danny wasn't sure whether he should hit her or laugh. She was delusional. There was no way he was seeing her again and certainly no way he was going to let her demand what she wanted. What was this some set up? Well, he was not a stooge. He stood up and began to dress. He reached down to pull up his pants and saw her grab for his wallet on the night stand. She opened it and pulled out his driver's license. He reached for her and she jumped away.

"You little shit. Give me that wallet. I'm getting out of here."

She took his license from his wallet and looked around for her pocketbook. He was enraged. How dare she steal his ID right before his eyes. He lunged for her. She kicked him in the balls. He lost his balance and tumbled back onto the bed. She quickly grabbed her bag. As he got off the bed he saw her put his license into her pocketbook. He jumped towards her and pulled his hand back. He sent his fist flying towards her as hard as he could swing. The punch caught her cheek. Her head jerked back and she stumbled backwards. As she fell her head caught the wooden corner of the chair by the bed. She went down in a heap. Danny stood over her breathing heavily. He reached down and saw that she was not breathing. When she hit the chair she must have broken her neck. He checked for her pulse. Nothing. She was dead.

The room began to swim. Danny was panicked, how could

this happen? It was an accident, he never meant to really hurt her. If she hadn't hit the chair she would be fine. He thought of calling the police. Hell, lots of the officers knew him and liked him. They might give him a break, but a murder in a motel room with someone he had just met was bad. And, as he looked at Monica he realized he would have a tough time explaining her split lip and the slight bruising on her neck and her arms. He also thought he might have broken her jaw with his last punch. That would not sit well with the cops no matter how friendly they were to him. Unfortunately, he knew enough about police work to know they would charge him with at least Manslaughter if not worse. He also had a moment of panic as he wondered if anyone would think to look back at Nora's death. To be tied to two women who died was not good. Danny was frantic. Of all the shit moments to have this happen, he couldn't believe he had been drawn into this mess.

He had to think fast. She had on her clothes, but not her coat or shoes. He struggled to put her coat and shoes on her. He buttoned her coat. He made the bed to look like only one person had slept in it. He knew that the motel operator had not seen her in the car when he checked in and he was hoping no one else had either. He cleaned up the room as best he could. He made sure he had all of her things and his things cleared out. He took his driver's license from her bag and put it back into his wallet which he put into his pants pocket. He opened the door. His car was still the only car in the lot. Luckily it was still early in the evening so the motel wasn't very busy. It was just starting to get dark. He got in the car, turned it around and backed it up to the door of the room. He jumped out and opened the trunk. He looked around quickly.

No one was in sight. He went back into the room and stood over Monica's body. He draped her pocketbook over her head.

Danny picked her up and carried her to the car. He folded her body into the trunk and locked it. He walked to the driver's side of the car and got into the front seat. He was sweating and breathing heavily. He checked to be sure there was no trace of her in the passenger seat. He prayed no one would see him drive away.

He drove slowly out of the motel parking lot. If the receptionist saw him leave he would think he was going out for dinner or a meeting. He would also see Danny was alone in the car. Danny's hands were clammy. He kept looking in the rearview mirror to see if he was being followed. Danny drove slowly down the street trying to figure out the best place to dispose of a body. He thought back to his conversations with the cops at the Glastonbury police department where he was an Auxiliary officer. Where had the cops said the best place to dump a body would be? Police discussed this type of thing all the time. Danny was desperate to remember where they described as the perfect place to dispose of a body.

Then it came to him. South of Hartford, along the river in Wethersfield was an abandoned sewage plant. The sludge that built up over the years was as toxic as anything you could find. The police always said that a body left there would be gone in days. Danny thought that was exactly what he had to work with: days. He drove carefully towards Wethersfield. When he reached the older section of the town where it became more industrial he turned down towards the river. He inched his way along the riverfront. The sewage plant was easy to find because the smell was disgusting. The disgusting odor also meant that there were no homes in the area. By now it was twilight and Danny had to find a spot to dump Monica. He saw a small opening in the vegetation along the sludge pond and stopped the car on the road above. He got out of the car and gathered some stones along the edge of the trees. The best way to be sure no one found Monica quickly was to make sure she sank into the sludge. He opened the trunk and put the stones into Monica's coat pockets. He hoped he collected enough stones to weigh her down so she wouldn't float to the top. He looked back and forth on the road to be sure no one was around. He scoped his hands under her body and managed to lift it over his shoulder. It took a few minutes but he carefully worked his way down to the edge of the pond and dropped her into the water. There was a slight splash, but she was still visible above the top of the sludge. He frantically wondered how he would get her further into the pond so she would sink.

He glanced around and saw a tree branch on the ground. He picked up the branch and used it to push her further into the sludge. The cops were right. It was disgusting. He watched as Monica McNally slowly sank into the ooze. He was covered in sweat and breathing heavily. He glanced around to see what the ground looked like. His shoe tracks were everywhere. He looked up and hoped the cloud cover meant rain. Rain would be perfect. Rain would erase his shoe marks in the mud and muck along the edge of the pond.

He went back to the car and tried to get the mud off his shoes. He put his head against the steering wheel and tried to think of what he should do next. This was not like Nora. He had time to think that one through. He planned it and was sure he had a great cover. This time he had to figure it out on the fly. The sad part was that this mess was an accident. He never meant to get rid of Monica, but here he was, hoping again that he wouldn't get caught. He took some deep breaths.

He turned on the car and headed to his office. It was after normal hours, but he hoped a few people would see him there and vouch that he had been working late that night. He wouldn't say anything to Ken until Ken called him. Eventually people at the trucking company would wonder where Monica went. Danny could honestly tell them that he left the bar with her and took her to the bus stop. He knew nothing about her and had no idea where she lived or where she went after she delivered Ken's message to him. Ken wouldn't want the police to know he was setting up poker games so Danny was pretty sure that his meeting with Monica would not come up. The other women in the office might wonder why Monica was sent to a bar with a note, but they wouldn't say much against their boss. They knew it would be better to be quiet about the strange girl who disappeared.

Danny pulled into the Penn Manufacturing parking lot just as it began to rain. Perfect. His shoe marks at the sludge pond would be obliterated. He thought he had dodged yet another bullet. Maybe he could relax. In fact, he had to relax. He was so keyed up that someone would think something was strange. Things were going too well in his life to have an idiot like Monica McNally mess up his future. He climbed the stairs to the front door of the building and headed to the men's room. No one was there so he grabbed a stack of paper towels and went into one of the stalls. He used the water from the toilet to clean his shoes. When they were clean he stuffed the used paper towels down into the trash can. The night cleaning crew had not arrived yet, so the dirty paper towels would be gone by the morning. He went to his desk. There were no other people in his area of the office so he took off his jacket, loosened his tie and sat at his desk, trying to control his breathing. About five minutes later one of the VPs wandered in and asked him why he was working late. Danny shrugged and said he just finished some paperwork that needed to get done and he was thinking about a new idea that he was working on. The VP smiled. Danny had a reputation of coming up with great ideas. It would be interesting to hear where this one was going. The VP said good night and left.

Danny tried to relax. He thought he could leave the building in about an hour. It would be hard to track where he had been that day so he had to think of the best alibi he could use if the police found Monica and linked her to him. He came up with a good story about leaving work to get his car fixed and trying to find a place that would work on a Cadillac. The repair shop he thought he would use was closed. That would work because he knew of a closed repair shop close to the bar where he met Monica. He could say he stopped in for a quick drink at the bar after he saw the shop had closed. If anyone saw his Cadillac in that part of town it would make sense. The bartender might mention him meeting with Monica but he could say he started talking with her and offered her a ride to the bus stop a few blocks away. Then he could say he came back to the office to finish up some paperwork. He thought the story would hold. Things would work out just fine if only he could get his hands to stop shaking.

What Danny didn't know was that when he and Monica came out of the bar, crossed the street and were getting into his car, Appolina was sitting at the traffic light at the corner. She saw them and slowed down to be sure she was seeing what she thought. Yes, it was Danny in his new fancy Cadillac and yes, that was a young girl with him getting into his car. The thin blond girl was most certainly not Dee. Appolina was beside herself. He was stepping out again. Poor Dee. Maybe it was time someone mentioned something to her. Why should Dee put up with how he behaved, or in this case, misbehaved. Appolina would go home and discuss it with Roberto. He would know the best way to handle this. The one person she would not discuss it with was her sister, Maria. She couldn't bear to hurt her sister or, just as likely, to hear her sister's endless excuses for Danny's terrible behavior. This was going to be between Dee, Danny and Appolina and no one else.

# October 17, 1953 – APPOLINA

Appolina waited patiently for Dee to arrive at her house. Appolina had offered to pick Dee up at her apartment if Danny wasn't around, but Dee said she had a friend who was always offering to drive her where ever she needed to go, so she would get a ride. She didn't want to bother Danny. He had been working very hard that week and wanted to spend Saturday with his pals hunting. The fall hunting season had just begun and the guys all loved getting their gear on and heading for the woods. Dee didn't even know what they would be hunting because she couldn't care less about the sport. She just knew that Danny loved it and it got him out of the house. He was proud of how good a shot he was. Over the years he had fashioned a small leather stool out of deer's feet from a kill and he had a taxidermist stuff a beautiful pheasant he had brought down. The pheasant was now in the place of pride in their seldom used living room.

Appolina was worried about the conversation she was planning to have with Dee. Roberto told her to go very slow and only bring up what she saw when Danny and the young woman walked out of the bar and got into his car if Dee seemed accepting. Roberto was worried this conversation would end in a full blown family war over what Appolina saw and surmised. He was afraid Dee would confront Danny,

Danny would go screaming to Maria that Appolina was spreading lies and Maria would side with Danny against Appolina. This could very well happen, but Appolina had seen too much and knew that as hurtful as the conversation would be for any wife, if she were Dee she would like to know the truth.

Dee arrived and let herself into the house. She took off her coat and hat and laid them over a chair in the living room. She heard Appolina making tea in the kitchen. She called out, "Hello," and headed for the back of the house where the kitchen overlooked Appolina's small garden. Dee looked around for Roberto, but Appolina explained he was out doing his Saturday haul at the local hardware store. Roberto was the ultimate fix-it man for everyone they knew. He loved helping everyone fix whatever needed fixing. He was always running out of specific size screws or nails and spent hours each weekend replenishing his work bench with supplies. Dee laughed and said she wasn't surprised. Roberto had already showed up at their apartment a few times to fix items that were broken. Appolina said she was grateful everyone used him so much. It they didn't she'd have to break things to make him happy. Both women laughed.

Appolina poured the tea from a delicate tea pot she bought years ago and put out some Italian cookies she made that morning. Dee settled into one of the comfortable kitchen chairs and Appolina sat across from her.

"So, Aunt Appolina, what is the big story you want to tell me? I was trying to guess what it was last night before Danny came home but I got nowhere. By the time we had some dinner and I cleaned up the kitchen it was too late to ask him if there was some big family news to share. He left for hunting early, so I'm still guessing. Is it a wedding? A new home? A new job?" Dee was smiling and looking directly into Appolina's eyes.

"Well, dear, it isn't really big news. That was just a small white lie so I could get you here with me for a chat." Appolina paused and looked out at the garden for a moment. The atmosphere in the room chilled noticeably.

"Did I do something wrong? Appolina, you have to know that I love you and your whole family so I would never deliberately do anything that would make you angry. Please tell me." Dee had reached out her hand and grabbed Appolina's free hand. She looked so worried.

"No, dear. This is definitely NOT something you've done. I am sorry to say it is something Danny has done and is doing." She paused and continued, "It's hard to have this conversation and if you want me to stop at any point, that would be fine. I don't want to hurt you. I am here to support you."

Dee pulled her hand back and nodded. In the back of her mind she had a feeling she knew what was coming. Things in her marriage were not going great. The relief she felt when Danny started traveling more and working later had changed into a coldness between them. She knew how much Danny liked sex and he was demanding it of her much less. She felt slightly nauseous thinking of Danny doing the things he did with her with other women. She braced for the news.

"Unfortunately, I've seen Danny with other women. Most recently on Thursday this week. He was leaving a bar with a young blond woman about 4PM. They got into his car and drove away. I have no idea where they went, but maybe it was an innocent meeting and I'm being horrible to think of any other reason he would be with someone else. Did he tell you he had a business meeting with a woman or some other reasonable explanation?"

Dee shook her head sadly. "No."

Appolina took a deep breath. "Did you know that Danny married you less than a year after his first wife and child died in that horrible accident?"

Dee's head shot up, "But he told me they had died quite a while before, I assumed it was years, and he had been so lonely when he met me. He missed them so much."

It was Appolina's turn to hang her head. "No Dee, Danny lied to us and told us he met you in mid -February. I knew it wasn't true because I saw you and Danny together shopping in G Fox & Company in January. Danny's family died in December, the 10th of December.

"But I met him in late November." Dee suddenly caught her breath and there was a deafening silence in the room. Dee realized what she had said and felt faint. She stood up and paced the small room. Appolina didn't move. Dee found her voice,

"Danny told me not to bring up the accident around his family because you and his mother were so upset you couldn't talk about it without breaking down. I never mentioned it to anyone because I thought it would cause so much distress. You all must think I'm horrible. What have I done?"

Appolina stood up and enveloped Dee in her arms. "You haven't done anything. I am sorry to be the bearer of such ugly news but Danny does not always tell the truth. He says what he wants you to believe. For what it's worth, I think he does love you. He was never very nice to his first wife and he wasn't very interested in his son. I think he was angry that he and Nora had to get married. Danny saw it as a trap. When he brought you to meet us he was very excited to get married. That was not how it was with Nora. It might not be what you believe but it was so different than his first marriage. He seems to want you, regardless of his side activities."

Dee didn't know what to say to that. Her head was spinning. A million thoughts were going through her brain. She thought of how often Danny was away now and how happy he was when they started dating only two weeks after his wife and child died! It made her sick. But, she married Danny and married people stayed married for life. Dee knew her marriage was stale and lonely. She would have loved to still want to be with Danny but there was no happiness when they were together. Maybe there would be a change over the years and she and Danny would grow closer. In the meantime, she was a Catholic. Catholics did not get divorced, they did not even discuss getting divorced. She could never go to her family and say she wanted to dissolve this marriage. Her mother and father might disown her and even Mary and George, who would understand best how difficult Danny could be would have a problem with a divorce. Would Dee be able to be a member of the church? Would she be able to receive the sacraments? It was impossible to imagine losing the entire religious structure of her life just because her husband liked to fool around with other women. She was sure she wasn't the first woman to go through this type of hell. She turned to Appolina,

"Appolina, I'm going to go home. I am so upset by all of this, but you have to understand, Danny is my husband, for better or worse. I am going to stand by him. If you really care for me promise me that this conversation will never be repeated to anyone we know. I never want Danny to know you told me and I never want my family or his family to know these awful things. Please promise me you will do this for me."

Appolina understood. If Dee was going to stick it out with Danny no matter what, she was right to keep this to herself. Appolina kissed Dee's forehead. "Yes, I promise. This is only between us. No one else has to know."

Dee walked into the living room and put on her coat and hat.

"Do you want me to drive you home?" Appolina felt so sorry for how Dee must feel.

"No, I would rather slowly go to the bus stop and make my way home. I need to be alone."

Dee left the house. She had to figure out how she was going to live the rest of her life.

# November 8, 1953 – DANNY

It had been three weeks since Danny disposed of Monica but he still found himself flinching when he heard police sirens. His palms would begin to sweat and he'd realize he was holding his breath until the sirens passed by. He was constantly looking over his so shoulder to see if anyone was following him. He wasn't sleeping well. He wondered how long he would feel this way. It was so different from how he felt after Nora. He had thought out how to deal with Nora and reasoned that it was the best alternative. He worked hard at the timing and the story the night Nora had her "accident". He was sure he was covered with his brothers, his business call and his performance at the funeral. With Monica it was different. He kept thinking of ways he would get caught. How the police might find the body. How the bartender would know they left together after having a drink. How someone would wonder why he was in a bar with Monica in the middle of the afternoon. How someone at the motel might have seen them entering the room together. He was a wreck wondering when her body would appear and he worried he couldn't explain her split lip, broken jaw or bruises.

He visited his friends in the Glastonbury Police Department more than usual. As a member of their Auxiliary Police group he was always welcome. He told them he had time to stop and visit because work was slow, and of course, he always supplied the booze and cigars for some conversation with the officers. He kept hoping he would find out if a body had been found. But they never mentioned it and he knew if a body mysteriously appeared in the area they would be talking about it. They might even remember that he was around when they discussed how perfect the abandoned sewage pond would be to dispose of a body. But so far, no word on any dead people in the area.

Ken called him once. He asked Danny if he had heard anything from Monica since he met her in the bar. Danny said no. He hadn't seen or heard from Monica since he dropped her off at the bus stop about three blocks from the bar the afternoon they met. Danny apologized to Ken that he hadn't gone to the poker games yet. He told Ken work had been very busy lately and he just couldn't get away. Ken said no problem and mentioned that Monica had not come back to work. Danny said he was surprised because while they were in the bar Monica described her job to him and seemed interested in what she was doing. Ken said she was young and might have had a better offer. She probably didn't know how to quit so she just stopped coming to work. He explained to Danny that it happened more often than you would think, especially with lower end jobs. Danny said he was sorry and hung up. He wiped his palms on his pants legs. He hadn't gone to the poker games or contacted Ken again.

Danny started coming home every night for dinner. Dee was surprised that he was living a normal schedule. After the first week it appeared he was going to be home for dinner all the time. Happy with this change, she went out of her way to make him nice suppers. Even in the bedroom when he wanted to have sex, it seemed more normal to her. He wasn't demanding she perform for him or making her do the things she hated. She was feeling much better about where they were as a couple. She wondered if Appolina had spoken to Danny about seeing him with another woman but thought it would be better not to bring it up. She knew she was married for life and since she wasn't going anywhere she was not going to complain. After six years of living what seemed to be a bizarre marriage, Dee began to think that their life was going to be OK. It was probably never going to be great, but Danny was a hard worker and when he was nice to her and normal in his work hours and comings and goings, she wasn't going to rock the boat.

Danny continued to work hard and visit the police station about once a week. Nothing had come of Monica's disappearance. He had a few run ins with some of the engineering guys at Penn Manufacturing, but his good ideas far outweighed the anger he stirred up with the staff. He felt he was still the golden boy in the CEO's eyes. It appeared that he was right in his assumptions. The CEO asked him into his office and told him he would be promoted at the end of the year to Vice President. He would be the youngest Vice President in the history of Penn Manufacturing and as of the beginning of the New Year he would have an office of his own and management would hire a secretary to handle his administrative work. Danny proudly told Dee that he was finally being recognized for his abilities. He hoped that the new position and prestige would make him stop worrying about bodies floating up from the sludge in Wethersfield.

# November 28, 1953 – DEE

D ee sat in the car staring out the window at the trees along the highway. She wondered how it had all gone so wrong. She and Danny had just had another knock down, drag out fight about nothing. The worst part was that they were not in the car alone. Mary and her four children were with them. The oldest boy, Andy, was sitting between Danny and Dee in the front seat and Mary was in the back with Dorothy, Joey and the 4 year-old baby, Audrey. The older kids had just finished their school year and they were all headed to Scranton to visit with Dee's parents, the kids' grandparents. George was supposed to be going on this trip, taking his wife and children in their own car, but at the last minute, George was offered overtime work at his job. The family needed the money, so Mary called Dee and asked if they could catch a ride with her and Danny. It was a simple request in Dee's mind. She and Danny spent a great deal of time with Mary, George and their children since they all lived in Hartford in walking distance to each other. Danny was used to the kids and they thought he was fun. Danny's big new Cadillac had plenty of room. The car was comfortable and the children were good travelers so it seemed logical that Danny could drive them all.

But lately Danny had been on edge and Dee didn't know why.

Things had been good for them for a few months last year. Danny spent more time at home and followed a normal schedule. When Danny was promoted at the end of last year he was happy and excited. He talked about them moving from the apartment into their own house. He wanted to know if she had anyplace she would like to go on vacation and most importantly, he spent more time with her. He talked about them moving into a house in the Hartford area. He said he was tired of living in an apartment. They went to the horse track and then to dinner or they played cards with George, Mary and other friends. For those brief months, Dee felt better than she had since they were married eight years ago.

But in the past three weeks the atmosphere changed. Danny began to complain again about his treatment at Penn Manufacturing. He said maybe he should think about finding another job. His complaining wasn't limited to the job. Suddenly he didn't like Dee's cooking, he thought she was slow at getting ready to go out, he was annoyed when she gave him the bills to pay and then annoyed when she didn't give them to him immediately. He had to work longer hours and do more traveling, which meant Dee wasn't sure when he would be home. Dee knew he had a new secretary, Evelyn. Dee wondered if Evelyn was pretty and was he was seeing her outside the office, but she pushed that thought away. Since Appolina talked to her about Danny's "girlfriends", Dee had taken a vow of silence on the subject. Appolina never brought it up again.

And now this scene in the car. Dee shuttered to think of what had just happened.

It started when Danny was mumbling something about trouble with the boss at work and Dee told him she couldn't hear him. He glanced at her with a menacing sneer and looked back to the road.

"You stupid woman," he screamed, "listen to me when I'm talking to you. You spend your time in a dumb cloud, never listening to me, well, you'll pay attention now."

Danny accelerated the car as fast as it would go. He was darting in and out of traffic and using his horn at anyone who was in his way. He took a curve very fast and threw everyone in the car against the door on the right.

Mary started to scream in the back seat, "Stop this right now. You'll kill us all."

Dorothy started to cry.

Danny screamed back, "I'll kill you all," as he jerked the car wildly into the other lane.

Andy began to shake. Dee looked down at him. He was pale and his eyes were shut tightly. He burrowed his head against Dee's arm. Both Dee and Mary were shouting at Danny to slow down. Dee leaned towards him, trying to grab the steering wheel.

"You're scarring the children. Stop this right now." He wouldn't listen.

The fast, hair raising driving went on. Danny passed trucks and cars without looking at who was coming towards them. He hit his brakes when he was about to rear end another car, which threw everyone towards the windshield. Mary pushed the little children down onto the floor in the back and Dorothy began to wail. Danny continued to drive at a break neck speed swerving in and out of the traffic. It was like he was angry that anyone could be in front of him. It went on for miles. Finally, on an empty patch of road he slowed down. Everyone in the car was breathing heavily.

Danny looked out his window and back to the road. He was now driving at the legal speed limit. His hands were wet on the steering wheel. He wiped them on his pants, one at a time. Dee could hear Mary comforting the children in the back seat. She pulled Andy's head from her arm and rubbed his back. He hadn't made a sound. They covered the final hour to Scranton without looking at anyone or speaking a word.

As they pulled up in front of the house in Scranton Dee jumped out of the car and walked quickly into the house. Mary gathered the children and herded them up the front porch stairs and into the front door. She carried the baby and gripped Joey's hand. Dorothy and Andy walked in front of her. When they were inside the house Mary let go of Joey's hand and put Audrey down. She walked to the phone and called George. He was home.

"Please come and get us on Sunday. We can't drive home with Danny. I'll explain later."

George was confused. They must have just arrived in Scranton. He couldn't figure out what could be the reason for him to drive all the way to Scranton to pick up Mary and the kids and drive them home. Weren't Danny and Dee driving home also? George started to question Mary, but he hesitated. There was something in Mary's voice that told George not to argue.

"OK. I'll be there Sunday by noon."

# October 5, 1957 – ALICE

A lice Keene sat at the small table in her favorite local café with her two best friends, Stanley Widdle and Hal Long. Alice loved spending time with these two guys. They were her friends and they were her confidants. At 28 years old, she didn't have many girlfriends, in fact, she had none. To Alice that did not matter. These fellows were better than girlfriends, they were soulmates. The three first bonded at the training classes for salesmen at the Underwood Typewriter Company. Alice had been the first female ever allowed to become a salesman for the company. Stanley and Hal had been the only guys in the class who were accepting, in fact, kind to her, as they went through the process of learning what they had to do to sell as many typewriters as possible to each customer. Alice made it into the class by accident. She was one of the best typists at Underwood which meant she was often asked to demonstrate a new machine for a customer. At a demonstration one afternoon, with an Underwood Vice President in attendance, she had to take over the entire presentation when the salesman who was describing the machine suddenly took ill. He ran from the room, trying to apologize to the group, but barely made it out before he vomited violently outside the door. The Vice President looked on in horror, but Alice kept calm. She stood up and closed the door just as the cleanup started outside and proceeded to finish the presentation for the clients. They were very impressed and so was the Vice President. That led to a discussion in the company about experimenting with a woman as a salesman.

There were a lot of men who were very unhappy about this development. Alice thought they were worried she would be better at selling typewriters because she could sit down during the sales presentation and type like the wind. It made the machine seem very easy to work. Hal and Stanley took the time to explain to her that the salesmen were much more worried that her beautiful long red hair, luminous green eyes and shapely figure would open doors to potential clients, most of whom were male, that the men could never crack. Oh well, for whatever reason, Alice had been a full-time salesman for the company for 2 years and she loved the job. She also loved the money it gave her to buy nice clothes, have her own apartment, and recently, have her own car. Alice was very proud of what she had amassed in the two years she was doing sales. The car was the ultimate sign of success for her hard work. There were very few women who had cars, and most of them had very old ones given to them by their father to help them out. Alice had purchased a new, shiny, Chevrolet. It was blue with beige interiors and she thought it was beautiful. She knew married women had cars that their husbands bought them to get the kids to school and do shopping. Alice felt she had achieved a milestone when she brought her car for herself. It was a moment of pride. It was also a strange moment when the car salesman asked her who would be paying for the car. She still chuckled at the look on the salesman's face when she told him she would be paying.

Alice couldn't believe how strongly her poor uneducated parents had argued with her about leaving their small farm in western Pennsylvania to go to a large city like Hartford where she knew no one and would be alone. They thought she would never survive. They were completely wrong, and Alice was thankful she had the guts to go against their wishes. She knew they cared for her and she dutifully sent them some money from each of her paychecks and tried to visit them at least twice a year. But life in Hartford, full of young people and growing businesses was much more fun than time on the dreary old farm.

Alice remembered how dull the farm and the small town a few miles down the road had been. She went to the local grammar and high school and earned great grades. Everyone thought she was quite bright, but Alice didn't think the people in the town would know if someone was bright or not. Most of them were uneducated farmers and some of them had never learned to read. Alice seized on the opportunity to learn typing during her senior year in high school. The school only had a few typewriters which were very old, but Alice managed to get to school early or stay late to practice. She figured she would need at least one skill when she left town that could land her a job. Little did she know that she would go from typing for a living to selling typewriters in such a short time.

Alice looked up as Hal was telling a story about a terrible sales call he made that day. She laughed at his impersonation of the general manager saying he couldn't care less if his typing pool women broke their fingers typing his orders. In fact, he saw no reason to upgrade his ancient machines until Hal gave him the statistics on how much more each girl would be able to type with the new machines. The statistics of course were made up, but the guy bought it completely, and Hal had a very good day filling the order sheet for the pathetic man. Alice had to laugh, she hadn't thought of making up statistics. That was what she loved about Hal, he had great ideas and he was totally willing to share them. He was free with all his tactics and thought it was great if Alice or Stanley tried his ideas. He wanted to know if his approach worked for Alice and Stanley like they worked for him. There was not a single selfish bone in Hal's body.

Hal, Stanley and Alice had formed a pact, of sorts, after they finished salesman training at the company. They decided to work together to increase their sales wins. They shared information, tips and most of all, ideas of what worked well and what did not to close a sale. They pitched in on doing research on upcoming companies in the area and shared their commissions. They had become a formidable team and since no one at Underwood had tried this teaming tactic before, the company did not know exactly how to treat them. Even though other salesmen complained about the Hal/Stanley/Alice team, Management decided to let them continue their approach. They were becoming the most successful salesmen Underwood had ever seen and anything that sold typewriters was good for Management.

It also helped that Hal, Stanley and Alice were completely comfortable working with each other. None of them was married, so there were no personal complications of men working with a woman, or anyone neglecting a spouse, and each of them was smart, young and hungry. They trusted each other with their thoughts and hopes even when it didn't involve selling typewriters. They were best friends. Alice also knew that Hal would do anything for her. Early in their partnership Hal and Alice had tried dating. Alice invited him to come to her apartment after a movie one night. It only took that evening to realize they would never be more than friends. Hal had a monumental crush on Alice and even thought he might be in love with her, Alice knew it would never work out. That encounter in her apartment after the movie had been illuminating. They kissed, rolled around on the bed and Hal took off Alice's bra, skirt and panties. But when it came to the actual moment of making love, Hal had only a limp dick. He tried and tried to stick his penis into her, but it was no use. In frustration, they turned away from each other and lay quietly in the bed. About fifteen minutes later, Alice slowly got up and put on her robe. Hal quietly pulled his clothes together. They walked to her front door and hugged good night. Alice had never been with a man who had a problem like that. She had no idea what caused it or what could be done about it. She thought it would be best to just not bring it up. Her work relationship with Hal was much more important than any one roll in the hay and the last thing she wanted to do was lose Hal as a co-partner. That part of their relationship was perfect. After going through a few uncomfortable meetings and never bringing it up, Hal seemed to realize Alice was never going to mention the disastrous night in her apartment. And since Hal was Hal, and certainly saw the value of their working relationship he wasn't going to mention it either. So, the friendship was back on track and Alice was grateful for it. She was sorry if Hal's problem was chronic, but then, she would never know because she was never going there again with him.

Stanley, on the other hand, had endless girlfriends and pals. He was always telling them about someone new he met and their entire background. Alice was sure that Stanley's success in the sales racket had a lot to do with how he could make people talk about themselves forever and seem interested in each person's personal details. He had a wonderful "gift of gab" and used it on everyone. Alice had learned a great deal from Stanley about asking questions, not talking too much and listening a lot.

The three of them decided early on that if they combined their information about everything to do with selling typewriters and the Underwood Company they would be ahead of the game. They shared info on sales tallies, new product development gossip, who was doing well and who was not doing as well and who the boss liked and who he did not. They exchanged information on growing companies in the city and how they could get into see the best clients. The friendship was important to each of them and they agreed that the key to making it work was that they would all, literally, WORK. There was no slacking and no letting down. They would help each other, but they would work as hard as they could to do well. They were the top three sales people in the division that year. They were feeling very good about themselves.

As they sat together at the café, they discussed the incredible increase in the number of employees at the insurance companies in town. The word was that Hartford wanted to become the "Insurance Capital of the World", and nothing needed typewriters more than insurance companies typing endless pages of insurance policies to collect premiums. They decided to do some research on the largest insurance companies and find out who was expanding the most. Hopefully it would lead to some great prospects.

After a quick dinner and a drink, Hal, Stanley and Alice called it a night. Alice had a big day ahead. She was scheduled to visit one of her best prospects to demonstrate a new typewriter they were marketing. She hoped the sales call would go well because this was just the type of client who would be growing over the years and nothing was better than having repeat clients. It was so much easier to make a sale to someone you already knew than starting from scratch each time and trying to get the initial sale done. Alice was already planning what she would wear and how she would do her hair for the visit. She was very meticulous in how she looked. She always wanted to be professional, but she also wanted to look attractive. She knew it all added up to helping her do well. She said good night to the guys and headed towards her car to drive to her apartment. It had been a great catchup with Hal and Stanley and she started thinking how she could get some of Hal's statistics into her meeting tomorrow to help bring home a sale.

The next afternoon, Alice drove her car into the Underwood Company parking lot at about 3:30 PM. She had just finished her sales call and was not sure it had gone as well as she hoped. The client was very cagey about what machines he needed and when he would need them. He asked endless questions about what the repair contract would look like, but then said he thought he could do better using an inhouse repair team. Alice tried to think of a way to introduce some positive statistics into her pitch, but the opening never came. She couldn't understand why the guy had taken the meeting if he was so disinterested in the product. He didn't even seem very interested in her. She had dressed carefully in a beautiful blue dress with white piping and had pulled her lush red hair back in a neat chignon. He hardly even noticed her face or her figure. Alice was used to men looking her over, even those who then got down to work and talked typewriters. This was a very different situation.

She parked the car in the Underwood lot and got out. She opened the trunk, pulled her handbag over her shoulder and pulled out the demonstration machine she had taken to the sales call. It was a little heavy, but she was used to lugging the machines around. As she walked towards the building, she noticed a tall, dark, very handsome man standing alongside a new Cadillac. He wore a beautiful double breasted blue suit, a very white starched shirt and a beautiful striped silk tie. He was smiling at her. He was between her and the door to the building. He stepped forward, put out his arms and said,

"Please let me carry that for you. It looks heavy. Is something wrong with it? Are you bringing it in for repairs?"

His voice was low and full. It sounded like a movie star, or a radio announcer. Alice let him take the machine from her arms and stood before him with her mouth open. He was gorgeous. His dark hair was perfectly trimmed and combed and his smile was radiant. She couldn't believe he was standing in the parking lot just as she drove up. Who was he and why was he there? He certainly did not work at the Underwood Typewriter Company. He stood in front of her waiting for her reply.

Finally, she found her voice,

"No, not for repairs, this is a new machine. I mean, it will be our new machine. I was just bringing it back to the office from a sales call."

He looked surprised,

"You're making sales calls?"

She straightened up and looked up into his face.

"Yes, I sell Underwood Typewriters."

"Well, I am impressed.... both with the company and with you. Congratulations.... that is, if it's going well. But something tells me from the looks of you that it is going very well."

Alice was not sure how to take this, but she thought he was complimenting her. She started towards the building and he followed with the typewriter in his arms. When they got to the door she opened it and he walked into the main reception area. Hal happened to be standing there talking to the receptionist. He turned and walked towards Alice and the good looking guy carrying her typewriter and smiled,

"Well, well, what have we here? Did you bring your client back to meet the whole team?"

Obviously, Hal thought the stranger was the client Alice had called on. She hesitated a second,

"Oh, sorry. No. This gentleman was helping me carry the machine into the building from my car. He is not the client I was with."

She turned to the man and thanked him as Hal took the machine from his arms.

"That was very nice of you. I appreciate your help."

The stranger smiled that dazzling smile at her again,

"No problem. My name is Danny Russo. And you would be?"

Alice finally found her voice.

"Oh sure, I'm Alice Keene and this is my friend and co-worker, Hal Long.

Danny nodded to Hal. Alice continued,

"Thanks again Danny I hope you have a nice evening."

He just kept staring at her face with her beautiful eyes and luscious lips. He finally said,

"It would be a lot nicer if I could have it with you."

Alice was shocked. Hal looked away and started to chuckle. Alice took a deep breath.

"Sorry, I'm not available this evening. But thanks anyway."

Danny smiled at her and nodded again to Hal.

"No problem. Another time. I'd love to hear about your sales work here. Seeing a woman in a sales position is a surprise. I hope I didn't offend you by being too forward."

"Oh no, not at all. Another time."

Danny smiled again and said,

"Goodbye Alice Keene."

He walked out of the building.

Hal, still holding the machine, turned to Alice. She was beautiful with her face slightly flushed and her eyes sparkling.

"Well that was interesting. He certainly was taken with you. And, from the look on your face, the feeling was mutual."

Alice looked down at the floor, then up to the ceiling. She had no idea what had just happened. Danny Russo had rattled her badly. Where did he come from? He didn't seem to be there for a meeting or for any purpose, he was just waiting. It made her curious in a strange way. And being around him made her feel helpless, like she wasn't in control. She didn't like it. But she did like him. Maybe she would see him again, or maybe she would never see him again. It was hard to tell what she wanted more. She leveled her gaze at Hal and said,

"Whoever he is I couldn't care less. I had a rough time with the client today and can't figure out what to do. Do you have a minute to talk about it?"

Hal nodded,

"Yes," but he didn't believe a word she said about Danny Russo.

# October 6, 1957 – DANNY

D anny eased into the car thinking how lucky he was. Just because his wimpy wife Dee asked him to drop off a sweater
she had borrowed months ago from a friend who worked at
the Underwood Typewriter Company, Danny met the gorgeous
Alice Keene. Dee worked at Underwood when they lived in
Hartford until about 2 years ago. At the time, Danny was a
rising executive at Penn Manufacturing, but that stint was
over now. Danny was let go from Penn over a disagreement
with the CEO. Penn Manufacturing still asked him to consult
with them from time to time when they needed him, but after
he lost his full-time job he and Dee relocated to New Jersey
where Danny picked up two new consulting jobs. One job was
with a candy manufacturer and one with a motorcycle maker.
The two jobs had nothing in common except that they both
involved manufacturing and Danny was a wiz at manufacturing issues.

The best part of being a consultant was that Danny could
come and go as he pleased. He often did the three-hour
drive from New Jersey to Connecticut. He wanted to keep
his contacts in the Hartford area. He was still working a few
days a month for Penn Manufacturing and he still saw his
former secretary at Penn, Evelyn, who was a diversion when
he was bored or needed a good fuck. He also liked visiting

Connecticut to see the guys at the Glastonbury Police Station. Years ago, Danny became good friends with some of the police officers in Wallingford, Connecticut, his hometown,. He got close to a few of the officers and learned they had a weakness for whiskey and cigars. It didn't take much to become their friend after a few well-placed "gifts" were distributed. It was very handy to have cops as friends when his brothers who were always getting into trouble needed a pass, or, more importantly, when his first wife and child had "accidentally" died in a gas leak at their apartment.

When Danny accepted his new job in Hartford at Penn Manufacturing, his Wallingford Police pals told him about a new police program in the town of Glastonbury, which was right outside of Hartford. It was called a Citizen's Auxiliary Police Force. Since Danny was moving to Hartford for a big job promotion and liked hanging around with policemen, the guys in Wallingford thought he would be great for the new program. They offered to recommend him. Danny liked being around cops and guns so he accepted the offer immediately. He had no idea what his life would be like in Hartford but being close to the local police had come in handy before and he liked the idea of knowing cops in the area in case he needed help in the future. In 1952 he attended the Auxiliary police training, passed the exam and shooting qualifications and was issued a pistol as he was sworn into the Glastonbury Auxiliary Police unit. Since then his interaction with the cops had revolved around some late-night card games and of course, more whiskey and cigars.

Back in 1953 Danny was very happy he knew the police in Glastonbury so well. That was the year he ran into Monica and had to deal with the debacle of her accidental death. Danny was finally over the anxiety and sleeplessness he had after that affair. He hated being so worried all the time and he knew that during those first few months when he was worried about the police finding and questioning him he acted strangely around his wife, coworkers and family. He was finally over the intense anxiety he had experienced after he'd dumped Monica into the sludge. Thankfully, that episode was over. Monica's body was never found, no one ever came to him to ask about that night and just recently he saw that the motel where Monica died had been demolished. As far a Danny was concerned, that episode was no longer an issue just as the accident with Nora and the baby were no longer an issue. He was once again a free man.

Today, Danny reasoned, there was something new his cop buddies could really help him with. He carefully wrote down the license plate number of Alice's car. He slowly drove out of the Underwood parking lot towards the police station. It had been a few weeks since he'd visited his pals, so this was a great time to catch up. As usual, the guys in the station were very happy to see him. He asked how things were and when they'd have some time for a card game. They all said next week would be fine, so Danny made a date. Just as he was about to leave he asked if it would be OK to check on something.

"I noticed just now when I was headed over to a Penn Manufacturing meeting that there was a new Chevy driving around with no brake lights. I tried to get the driver's attention, but no luck. Can we find out who owns the car? The driver looked like a kid who probably doesn't know what a brake light is. I managed to get the plate number before the Chevy pulled away. Maybe I could contact the parents and give them a heads up. You know I never actually get to do any police work with you guys. This might be my big chance."

The officers all laughed. It wasn't exactly police policy to let Danny follow up on a traffic report but it was exactly the kind of work they all hated, very boring and usually a total waste of time. Besides, before Danny contacted the parents there was a good chance some patrol car would have already spotted the defective lights and stopped the Chevy.

The senior officer looked at his guys, who were all smiling and nodding, and then at Danny.

"Sure, I guess we could run the plate number and give you an address. But remember, if you do contact someone, be sure to show your ID and say it is a curtesy call. We can't have an Auxiliary policeman making any statements as to the law."

Danny immediately agreed.

"Absolutely. I wouldn't be surprised if my entire interaction amounted to a note on these people's door. I'll be sure to let you know what happens, no matter what and, if it turns out to be interesting, I'll have to furnish the refreshments for next week's card game."

Danny gave them all a big wink and the junior guy went off to run the plate number amid a chorus of chuckles. By 5:15 that evening Danny was in good shape. He called Dee to say he was held up at Penn and would not be home until the next day. Then he called Evelyn to say he could not see her that night because he had an urgent meeting early the next day in New Jersey. He promised to be back the next week and call her. He drove to Alice's apartment and parked in front of her building.

# October 6, 1957 – ALICE

A lice parked her car a few doors down from the front of her apartment building. It wasn't a very large complex, just six apartments, three on each side, with a central stairway. It was a three-story red brick building, built right after the war, so it was very new. She was proud of how lovely the tree lined street was and how well she was living. With these happy thoughts she headed to the front door. It had been a strange day with the weird presentation and then meeting this Danny Russo, but Hal had talked her through the issues with the client and got her excited about the follow up. As he said,

"Some prospects want to be wooed, and sometimes those turn out to be the best and longest customers because when you finally get them to say yes to an order they have put you through the wringer and feel you earned the business. As long as you service them well from then on they use you forever."

Alice liked this advice and decided she would call on the difficult client again tomorrow with some follow up information on the repair and service contracts they could fashion for his needs. As far as Danny Russo was concerned, he might never appear again, so he could be easily dismissed.

Suddenly, Danny Russo was standing in front of her. She was too shocked to speak. She swallowed and tried to clear her throat.

"Why are you here?"

She whispered.

Danny responded with his trademark smile.

"I thought I should check to see if you're still busy tonight. Just a chance, but worth the try. What do you think?"

Alice was too confused to know what to do. He was so alluring, but how did he find her and what should she say? This was way beyond anything she had ever experienced. Suddenly the farm in Pennsylvania seemed very far away. On the other hand, she didn't come to Hartford to live a life like on the farm. She came to have new experiences and Danny certainly represented a new experience to her. He looked rich and he acted strong and she was very intrigued. She decided she wanted to know him and she wanted to see what it would be like to be with him. In fact, maybe he was going to be the best thing that ever happened to her. She straightened her shoulders and look up into his face.

"Want to come up for a drink? Then I can decide if I am still busy tonight."

He smiled at her and held out his arm towards the door of the building for her to lead the way.

Alice put her purse on the small table inside her apartment door. She gestured for Danny to go into the living room. It was neat but sparse, furnished with a small sofa, coffee table, one side lamp on another small table and a chair. There was a blue rug on the floor and most of the furniture was covered in a small rose print fabric.

"Very nice," Danny said.

"Thank you. How about that drink. Is scotch OK?"

He nodded yes.

"And please add some ice if you have it. "

"Of course."

She left to get the drinks. Danny looked around the room and was glad to see there were no pictures of young men anywhere. There was one picture of an older couple he took to be her parents. They were simple, hard-working people from the looks of it. Danny could relate to that. He could also relate to her ambition. He was nothing but ambitious in everything he did, but he was startled to realize that he found Alice's obvious ambition, her elevated job for a woman, her living by herself, and her new car, very alluring. He wasn't sure he had ever met a woman who seemed to have it so together. He had a wife who was attractive, but after ten years, any excitement between them was gone. Dee was a nag and dull and uninterested in what he wanted to do or how he wanted to get ahead. He had gone through a lot to woo her and win her, but after the first few years the relationship was boring, especially in the bedroom. He also had his young secretary, Evelyn, whenever he wanted but he could see that would end soon. When he started to see Evelyn she was willing and fun, but now she was worried about her husband discovering their meetings and her position at Penn Manufacturing since Danny left the firm. More and more of their time together was taken with Evelyn worrying about how other people looked at them and if anyone would ever alert her husband or Danny's wife about what was going on. Danny wasn't sure how it would end with Evelyn, but he could figure it out. Maybe he'd just get more and more busy in New Jersey and not be able to come to Harford as much. How would Evelyn know the difference if he was in town for Alice? Yes, Alice. Alice was so beautiful.

He had to figure out how this could work. He had a lot going on, but on the other hand, he wasn't going to let this go. Alice was terrific.

She returned with the drinks in her hand. He took his and offered her a seat on the sofa. She sat down and crossed her beautiful legs. He imagined touching her long calves and moving up to her thighs. He thought of how luscious it would be to stroke her clit. He sat down next to her and tried to get a grip on his lust. This was unbelievable.

Alice leaned forward to put her glass on the coffee table. She felt Danny's hand on the back of her neck and froze. She did not move. Danny's hand went to her hair and undid the chignon she carefully set that morning for work and her presentation. Her freed hair fell forward, veiling her face. Danny pushed her hair behind her ear and stroked her cheek.

"What are you doing?", she said.

"I am making love to you."

She looked at him sideways. He was perfect. She couldn't deny it. Her last experience with sex had been with Hal which she had to admit was less than satisfying and Danny looked like he could never have a Hal problem with any woman.

She sat up and turned to him. It was no use. She wanted him. She was 28, unmarried and free. Why not?

Danny leaned into her and she fell back on the sofa. He came at her mouth, but it was really her face. He devoured her lips, her cheeks, her ears, her forehead. He kissed her everywhere. She was breathless. She pulled him closer and felt his weight on her. He pushed off and pulled her to her feet. They headed for the bedroom and he began to strip her of her clothes. She helped him. They got off her shoes, dress, stockings, garter and bra. He pulled down her panties as she began to unzip his pants. He pulled off his jacket and tie and worked on his shirt. She pulled it back as he finished the last button and pulled up his undershirt. His chest was full and had a thick patch of black hair down the middle. The hair went all the way to his underwear and disappeared. He pulled the pants down and she saw his huge erection. They went down on the bed together.

Alice couldn't believe what he did. She was not a virgin, but never had she been so consumed. He licked and kissed her everywhere. He bit her nipples gently, which drove her wild. He rubbed her clit and penetrated her with his finger. Then two fingers. It sent shivers through her. Then he pulled her on top of him. This was so new she couldn't figure out what to do. He laughed and told her to just enjoy herself. He used his finger to play with her as she sat on him.

He loved every bit of it. With her on top he could see her gorgeous body, those fabulous tits and her tiny waist which he could surround with both hands. Her skin was soft and creamy and her bush was as red as her hair. He came in a sudden spurt. It was more than he could ever have imagined. He immediately knew he wanted this to go on for a long time. She slumped against him, breathing heavily.

"Take a break, honey. We're just getting started."

She smiled at the low slow voice. She really liked it.

They spent the night in bed. He insisted they order out for a pizza delivery about 10:30, but after the pizza break, the sex continued. The next morning, Alice did something she had never done before, she called in sick for work. Stanley called her home to be sure she was OK. She said she was but had a bad headache and hoped it wouldn't turn out to be something worse. She said she was spending the day in bed. Stanley agreed that was the best and said he would check in on her later. She asked him to tell Hal so he wouldn't worry and so he wouldn't call. She told Stanley to pass a message to Hal that she intended to catch up with the difficult client the next day when she felt better. She told Stanley she was hoping to sleep most of the day and didn't want to be woken. He said that would be the best thing for her to do. She hung up the phone and walked back into the bedroom. Danny was drinking a cup of coffee he made and offered her some.

"Next time we'll go out for breakfast, sweetheart, but not today. Today I get you all day to myself. "

Alice smiled. She could do this for a while.

# November 15, 1957 – ALICE

A lice was happy that Hal and Stanley were free to come to her apartment that evening. She had a lot to discuss with them. The past five weeks with Danny had been both exciting and disturbing. But, she had to admit that the disturbing had taken over the exciting and not in a good way. She wanted some advice and maybe some help. She knew her friends would do whatever was needed.

Initially Danny had been fantastic. He managed to see her every three or four days and said he had business to do the other days. The disturbing part of the relationship was that when she asked him about his business there were no clear answers. He always had a one-word answer that told her nothing and then he quickly diverted the conversation to other topics. He was fun and handsome and amazing in bed, but she knew very little about him. At first she let it slide, but when it continued she began to get suspicious.

To begin with, Danny could never explain why he was in the parking lot at Underwood Company when she met him. He also never really said what his work was and why he could appear randomly from time to time at her apartment in Hartford, and stay for a night or more, and then disappear for a few days. She couldn't figure it out. She had a job that demanded her time each working day. To her having a job was like clock-work. Danny never mentioned the name of the company he worked at or what he did. He seemed to have endless cash which he used to take her to dinner, the movies and clubs for dancing, but never seemed to need to be at work. He also never spoke about his family. If she asked, he said he hardly ever saw them and that he was from a no name town in Connecticut that she had never heard of, except he never gave her the name of the town.

Most disturbing was that he was intensely jealous of her friendship with Hal and Stanley. Initially she thought he was just being possessive, but in the last few weeks he was angry and volatile if she mentioned them at all. He lashed out at her for "needing them around", and said she should have girlfriends, not boyfriends. He told her to stop talking to them about her business and what she did in her off time. He screamed at her a few nights ago because she mentioned the work Hal and Stanley were doing with her to contact growing businesses in the Hartford area. Danny flew off the handle and told her the men were taking advantage of her. They would never share information equally with a woman. He threw a cup across the room and it broke into pieces as it hit the sink. She backed away in horror staring at the shattered cup in the sink. She slowly looked up at him, turned and walked into the living room. She sat on the sofa with her face buried in her hands. All she could think of was how big and strong he was and how helpless she was. He had suddenly become a monster. She was scared.

Danny came into the room, sat on the sofa next to her and brushed back her hair. He tried to pull her close, but she pushed away from him.

"Listen baby, I'm sorry about the cup, but you have to understand that I'm not used to having a woman who is close to other men. I mean, I am crazy about you and it seems you spend more time with those two guys and talk more about what you are doing with them than with me. I just want to be with you all the time," he said.

She had to think quickly. She wasn't sure that Danny was over his rage, or that he wouldn't fly off the handle again. She had to tread carefully with this situation. She tried to paste a smile on her face, but it was very weak.

"Ok. I understand," she lied. Then she let him hug her and pull her into the bedroom. For the first time in their relationship, the sex didn't feel so good to her. He left in the morning. She was relieved.

She thought the situation might calm down if they took a break from each other so she told Danny she was planning drive to Pennsylvania to see her parents over the next few days. Danny seemed to accept this and told her he would be back in about five days to see her.

Two days ago, Danny spent Thursday night with her. In the morning, before she went to work, he took her to a small coffee shop in downtown Hartford for breakfast. While they were eating, a young, lanky boy of about 12 walked into the coffee shop. The kid had a large newspaper delivery pouch over his shoulder with the words, "The Hartford Courant" across the front. He went to the counter to order a donut, paid the waitress and turned looking directly at Alice and Danny. The kid had just taken a bite of his donut and suddenly stopped chewing. He swallowed hard and blurted out,

"Uncle Danny?"

Alice looked at Danny who had a shocked expression on his face which he quickly covered. He smiled at the kid and said,

"Andy. How are you? Did you just finish your route? This is my secretary, Alice. We're headed to work early so we thought we'd get some breakfast."

Alice as aghast. She had no idea what was going on, but Danny sounded as guilty as hell. She couldn't believe that he called her his secretary, and it was obvious that if this kid was Danny's nephew, Danny had family in the area. Family he never talked about and denied he ever saw. What was going on? Why did he lie?

"Bye," the kid waved quickly and left the coffee shop.

Alice got up to leave. She wasn't staying here to hear the story that went with this scene. Danny suddenly caught her wrist in a vice grip. He was so strong that he pulled her back into her chair by bending her wrist. She winced in pain and looked him in the eye. He had the angriest face she had ever seen. He was practically snarling at her. She loudly said,

"Let me go. You are hurting me."

Danny glanced around the coffee shop to see if anyone had heard her. A few people looked at them, but no one moved.

"Sit down now." His voice was steely.

She sat back in the chair and stared at his large hand encircling her wrist. He looked down at her hand which he had pinned to the table and looked back at her. His face relaxed and he let her wrist go.

"Come on Alice, the kid is the son of a friend I don't see

much anymore. I had no idea he had a paper route around here."

"He called you 'Uncle Danny," she said.

"Yes, but we're not related."

"Really? Why did you call me your secretary? Why didn't you introduce me as your friend?"

"Alice, a kid like that knows what a secretary is but not what a friend is. It's better this way."

Alice was going to object but thought better of it. She needed to get to work and her wrist was very sore. She did not want Danny to erupt again. Her first instinct was to get away from him as quickly as possible.

"Look, could you drive me to my car? I need to get to work. I have an early meeting today with my supervisor so I don't want to be late." She tried to sound normal but wasn't sure he was buying it.

"Sure, I'll pay the bill and we'll go."

Danny threw some bills on the table and they stood up to leave. He put his hand on the small of her back and directed her out the door and to his car. They didn't speak as he drove her the short way to her apartment. He pulled up behind her car and she opened the door to get out. Suddenly he grabbed her arm and pulled her back. She tried to look down and not at him, but he lifted her chin so he could see her eyes.

"I'll be back on Monday, honey."

She got out of the car and tried to walk calmly to her car. Her hand shook so much it took her three tries to get the keys into the ignition. He had rattled her badly. She wasn't sure what he meant by "back on Monday". She hoped he thought they could pick up where they left off the night before, but there was something threatening in his voice that was making her very anxious.

Alice thought about the coffee shop incident, along with all the other uncomfortable signs she was picking up around Danny and decided that she needed to share this with friends she trusted. She needed advice and she needed support. She was scarred. She was hoping Hal and Stanley would make some sense of this guy. She was a bundle of nerves.

Thirty minutes later sitting on her sofa, Alice had related to Hal and Stanley the entire Danny story. When she finished the men were both were staring at the floor. Alice had a sinking feeling in her chest. They didn't look hopeful. Finally, Stanley started talking,

"This Danny guy is violent, secretive, lying and threatening. He doesn't want you to see us but he does want you to be available whenever he feels like showing up. He won't tell you what he does or anything about his background. He won't introduce you as his girlfriend and he won't even tell you why he was sitting outside your workplace when you first met him. And he managed to find your address within two hours of meeting you and show up at your house. This guy has resources and we have to find out what they are."

Alice was mortified. When it was put like that it sounded horrible and made her seem very stupid. Alice did not think she was a stupid person. In fact, she prided herself on being somewhat crafty. Well, so much for crafty, Danny had made a fool of her. And worse, he was coming back. It didn't sound like she could just tell him that the relationship was over. She looked at Hal and Stanley and wondered what she could possibly do.

Hal spoke up,

"I think we need to know more about Mr. Russo. It seems to me that he will continue to bother you until he is either tired of you........,"

Alice's eyes widened. She stared at Hal,

"Sorry but it will probably happen,' he continued, 'Or you find a way to scare him off. Personally, I saw how he looked at you that first day in the reception area so I would go for the scare him off scenario, it will be awhile until he gets tired and moves onto another young girl."

"But how can I possibly scare him? He's stronger and quicker and I am the one who's scared!"

"I know, Alice, but there are ways to scare someone that don't involve manhandling them or threatening them. Let's think about how we learn more about Danny Russo. We research companies all the time, how hard could it be to research a person."

For the next hour Hal and Stanley threw out ideas and thoughts about Danny Russo. What they knew was his license plate was from New Jersey. He had some family in the area. He did not have a normal nine to five job. He was at the Underwood building two months ago with apparently no connection to the company. He was coming back on Monday.

Based on their conversation, they came up with a plan. It was hard on Alice. They were sure the only safe way to get rid of Danny was for Alice to go along with him until they had some information they could use. Alice reluctantly agreed because she knew she had to do something. She was frightened of Danny, but she was also mad. She couldn't believe that after almost two months or being so happy he managed to make their relationship ugly. She wanted to get away from Danny, but she was hungry for revenge. He was not a nice person and she wanted him to know that she was not some babe he could push around. The friends planned to meet again on Tuesday after Alice gave them the all clear sign that Danny was gone.

Monday was not as bad as Alice thought it would be. Danny came to see her. They ate a quick supper he brought with him from a local Deli and then made love. He told her he had to leave that night because of a business meeting the next morning in New Jersey. She acted sad and said she'd miss him. He seemed satisfied. Before he left he said he'd take a quick shower. As soon as she heard the water go on she went through his pockets and found his wallet. His license gave her his address in New Jersey which she wrote down on a piece of paper and slipped it into her underwear drawer. She also found his Glastonbury Auxiliary Police ID card. There was no other information on his life, but she felt she had something to report the next day.

On Tuesday Hal and Stanley met Alice at a small restaurant in her neighborhood. They also had news to report. Stanley had sweet talked the receptionist at Underwood about the very handsome man who had come to the Company two months before. It took her awhile to remember Danny, but when Stanley mentioned that Hal and Alice had been talking with him in the reception area, she remembered the day. She thought it was strange that he had been into the building to drop off a package, left, and then came back in with Alice. She thought Alice and Hal knew the man because they were all talking together. Stanley asked why Danny had come and the receptionist remembered that he dropped a package off for one of the women who worked on the assembly line. Stanley thought that sounded strange since Danny looked like an executive type. Why would he be giving something to someone who worked on the assembly line? The receptionist remembered the assembly line woman's name and Stanley went off at lunch time to find her.

"And, low and behold, the woman knew exactly who I was talking about. She had never met Danny, but he dropped off a sweater she had loaned to his wife when she worked at Underwood."

Alice looked stricken,

"His wife?"

"Oh yes. Danny's wife worked at Underwood Company on the assembly line and was a very good friend of the woman I spoke with. One day the wife wasn't feeling well and was cold, so the friend lent her a sweater she never wore that was in her locker. Danny's wife left the company a few months later because Danny had a new job in New Jersey. When the wife unpacked in New Jersey she found the sweater and asked Danny to bring it back to Underwood with a note thanking the friend. One mystery solved, Danny was never going to tell you about his family because he might have to mention that he had a very inconvenient wife to deal with."

"But, I don't understand,' said Alice, 'why does Danny come back to Connecticut so much? Doesn't he have to be at his job in New Jersey?"

"I asked the woman about that, but she said that Dee, Danny's wife, always said she couldn't understand her husband's work. He was in some sort of manufacturing and came and went all the time. I think he is a consultant, so he makes his own hours and, obviously, gets paid well for what he does."

Alice thought about this for a minute. It began to explain his coming and going and his "business meetings" which was the only time he seemed to take his work seriously. His having a wife was a blow. It never occurred to Alice to ask if he was married before she took up with him. It made her feel like a country bumpkin. She should have realized an attractive man of that age could be married. Of course he could have a family that he returned to when he left her. And of course, he never wanted to tell her where he lived or who his family was. What was she thinking? Why hadn't she insisted he give her more information? Now she had another reason to be angry with Danny the low life who cheated on his wife. She wondered if there were children. It made her sick to think there could be a daughter, son, or more who he was deserting while he slept in Alice's bed. Hal and Stanley looked at her as she ran through these thoughts. Her face was red.

"Are you all right? You look angry."

"Damn straight I'm angry. This guy is disgusting. What if he has children too?"

Hal and Stanley looked at each other and back at Alice.

"Look Alice. You can get as mad as you want, and the madder the better when we figure out what we can do to expose this guy, or better yet, to hurt him back. In the meantime, we need to quickly find out all we can about him because the sooner we get something on him that keeps him away from you, the better off you will be. Then you can enjoy being as angry as you want."

Alice hung her head. They were right. She took a deep breath and continued,

"I found out something too. Danny is a member of the Glastonbury Auxiliary Police Department. I saw his police ID in his wallet."

Hal started to laugh.

"That explains how he got your address. He must have had his pals at the police station run your license plate through their records. Didn't you say that you drove into the parking lot when you first saw him? So, he knew your car."

"Yes, he saw me get out of it. It was parked close to his."

"Another mystery solved." Said Stanley.

They decided they now had some things to go on. Hal would see if he could have a conversation with some of the officers at the Glastonbury Police station about their Auxiliary Policy group and how Danny Russo got involved with them. Stanley said he would try to find some information on a Danny Russo as a consultant. They agreed Alice would keep up the charade with Danny until they had a plan.

Two days later Stanley asked Hal and Alice to have lunch with him outside the office. They met in a small sandwich shop about a half mile from the Company. Stanley had just finished a business call to a company called Penn Manufacturing, and what he had heard was unbelievable.

While waiting in the reception area for his meeting to start Stanley over heard two women talking about an Evelyn Smith who worked at Penn. The women were saying that Evelyn had just been assigned to another Vice President as a secretary. This was the second Vice President she was supporting and she was not happy. Apparently Evelyn used to work for only one Vice President, but ever since that Vice President left she kept being assigned to other people. She was upset because every now and then the old Vice President reappeared in his new consulting role with the company and loaded incredible amounts of work on her. With her new assignment and the old guy giving her work when he showed up, she was overwhelmed.

Stanley thought this was typical secretarial gossip until he heard the next comment which made him sit up and really listen.

"Of course, I don't think it has anything to do with the work load. Evelyn is just angry that when Danny Russo shows up she has to spend time with anyone else. And by spending time, you know what I mean." The first woman nodded knowingly to the second woman.

The two women moved away from Stanley. He frantically thought of something to say to them to learn more.

"Excuse me, I'm Stanley Widdle, I was sitting here and I think I just heard a name I haven't heard in a while. Does Danny Russo still work here?" Stanley asked the women with the sweetest smile he could muster.

"No, Danny left about two years ago, but he comes back from time to time to consult with the higher ups. He didn't leave on good terms, but the work he does is supposed to be great, so they made him a consultant. He was here last week. Do you want us tell him you were looking for him?" One of the women was searching Stanley's face for a reaction.

"No, probably best you not mention my name or that I was asking. You see, I used to be great friends with his wife, Dee. I knew she wasn't in the area any more and when I heard his name I wondered if they'd moved back. But I guess not if he comes and goes. I think they moved to New Jersey."

The other woman jumped into the conversation,

"Yes, they did go to New Jersey, but believe me, his wife would not be happy to hear the time he spends here with Evelyn Smith, his former secretary. Best you not mention it to her. "

Stanley nodded knowingly, looking sadly at both women. His demeanor seemed to say, "how awful can a man be" and the two women nodded knowingly back at him. Just then, he was called to his meeting and he thanked them both for the information and wished them a nice day.

As in most of Stanley's meetings, he made instant friends with the guys in the room. They seemed quite willing to work with Underwood for some of their machines and Stanley said he'd be happy to follow up with them when they were ready. As the meeting broke up, Stanley mentioned hearing Danny Russo's name as he was waiting for the meeting to start. One of the guys, named Sam, asked Stanley how he knew Danny. Stanley said he didn't know him, he only knew of him.

"And, actually, what I know is not very nice. He sounds like a tough character."

Sam quickly jumped in,

"You have no idea. The guy stole every thought anyone had around here and blamed all his mistakes on others. He was caught paying off someone to keep quiet about his stealing others' work and rumor has it that he chases every skirt he sees. Everyone thinks he is banging his former secretary. He's known for his gambling and not paying off quickly when he loses. He's always in a money hole but lives large. I don't know if he has a friend left at this place."

"Now wait a minute, Sam", the other man stepped forward. "This is internal stuff, Stanley doesn't need to hear about our dirty laundry.

Stanley agreed and thanked the men again for their time. Immediately after his meeting he called Hal and Alice to meet him for lunch.

"A wife and a mistress? Really? Stealing from coworkers and trying to pay them off? Gambling? Am I the dumbest woman on the planet?" Alice was livid. The stories about Danny got worse and worse. And, in addition to his antics with her, he was also having sex with another woman. She was disgusted.

Hal was intrigued. In his mind this guy redefined scum bag. And the fact that he was volatile and threatening made it more important that they get rid of him without his knowing what they knew. Hal tried to reassure Alice.

"Well, he seems to like you best, Alice, if that helps, but what is unbelievable is this guy is doing all of these horrible things and has pals at the police station. Give me a day or two and we'll figure out what comes next."

The next day Hal asked Stanley to meet him right after work. They sat in Hal's car, rain pouring outside, and he reported on his trip to the Glastonbury Police Station that morning.

"You know, mornings are great in police stations. The day hasn't really taken off yet and the cops are all lounging around with their coffee. Luckily, a guy I know is great friends with an officer, Jim Macey, who works at the station and told me to look him up. Jim was at his desk and offered me a seat while we chatted. I got around to asking about their Auxiliary police program. He said they had instituted it a few years ago and had about ten men enrolled. I asked if the men were former army guys or policemen. He said not really. They were all from different backgrounds. In fact, they had a doctor in the group and a very successful businessman. I acted surprised and asked why the businessman was part of it. He began to talk about this Danny Russo, a bigshot at Penn Manufacturing, who was recommended by the Waterbury Police Department. Seems Danny is originally from Waterbury and befriended a few officers at that station over the years. I asked if there was a reason Danny was so interested in police work. Jack said that he wasn't sure, but everyone feels Danny has had a rough time. His wife and young child died in a gas leak accident in Wallingford about ten years ago. The Wallingford policemen said Danny took the death very badly. He had since remarried, but no kids with the new wife.

Hal continued, "Knowing that Danny's wife, Dee, worked in Hartford, I researched their names in the Hartford papers for a wedding announcement. Danny married Dee one year after his wife and kid died." Hal took a deep breath and continued,

"So, Danny not only has a wife, mistress and our Alice, but also had another wife and child who conveniently disappeared from his life one year before he married his current wife. I can't help but think that is a bit too convenient. I think Danny is a bad guy. I am wondering if he had something to do with his first wife's "accident" and if he is used to picking up women, romancing them and then getting rid of them. It is frightening. And I'm sorry to say it doesn't sound like the police have a clue as to how he operates. He has managed to con them all."

Hal looked at Stanley. They both knew this was too much for Alice to handle. She was plenty angry at Danny and he had manhandled her already, but if the guy was also a murderer it was more than she could take. They had to figure out a way to get her away from him as quickly as possible. This was no longer a situation of getting the guy to leave Alice alone. It was now an all out press to get Alice safely away from him.

Stanley piped up, "Let's go see Alice, but let's not share this police info with her."

They met later that evening at Alice's apartment. Hal and Stanley were trying to warn Alice that she had to be careful around Danny without getting into the specifics of what they found out.

"Alice we'll work it out. We know so much more than he would ever tell you, so we're in a good position.

Alice didn't look convinced.

"Ok, so what do we do? We have dirt on Danny but he is still planning to see me later this week." She was almost crying.

Hal suddenly smiled.

"Can we meet tomorrow night? I've been hatching another plan and if we can get Danny Russo to help us carry it out so much the better."

It was late and they all had a heavy work day ahead so they agreed to meet the next evening at their favorite bar.

The plan Hal laid out for them while they ordered beers and burgers was so convoluted and complicated that both

Stanley and Alice had a hard time following it. Hal assured them that Danny was no dope and they needed to lure him in a very sophisticated way. To Hal's way of thinking, Danny was dangerous as long as he was around, but Danny was also a means to an end. And like so many of Hal's ideas, this one was well thought out.

Hal explained that he had been thinking about how the three of them were doing and what was happening in their industry. Yes, they were making great money at Underwood and as the three top salesmen they could keep doing it for a long time. But Hal thought they could be even more successful as a sales team in a much larger company with more products to push. So he researched where their industry was going. He discovered a growing company in California called Hewlett Packard that was making the next generation of office machines which would dwarf anything Underwood Company ever considered manufacturing.

"Wouldn't you love to live in California? Wouldn't you love to make really big money with a company that is changing our industry? What will we do if Underwood never gets with the modern tide? There are already rumors that the company may be for sale. Are we going to sit around making good, not great money until Underwood disappears?" Hal was at his most persuasive selling moment as he pushed the idea of them leaving together for the West Coast.

"Ok, Hal,' said Stanley, 'but moving to the West Coast takes money for travel, to set up apartments and to job hunt and I don't think any of us has that much saved up. I know I don't."

"That's where Danny comes in. The best way to get back at

Danny is to take his money in a crooked scheme. We know he played fast and loose with the truth at Penn Manufacturing, and even though he is obviously very talented, they let him go. It must have been bad. But, not so bad that they don't want him around for consulting from time to time, which means he must be very smart.

We can't go at him for his infidelity because everyone seems to know about it but the women he is involved with. If confronted he would simply deny it. We can't go at him for his antics at Penn because he's already been fired for them and as far as we know he hasn't done anything against the law and he's got friends on the police force. The only way to get at Danny Russo is in his pocketbook. And I think we can convince him to get into an investment which will be sure to reap some money. But not for him, for us. And we can get him involved in a shady way so that when it goes bust and he loses his money he can't go to the authorities because he shouldn't have been in the investment to begin with,"

"I would do anything to hurt him. I hate him." Alice quietly said.

"Ok, I'm in." Stanley assented.

Hal turned to Alice and took her hand.

"Alice, you're the key. Here's what you tell him when you see him. And it would be very good if you could make it seem like he must agree and come up with the money quickly. We don't want him to start snooping around to see if the deal is real."

For the next hour Alice listened carefully and parroted back everything Hal said. By the end of the night she thought she was ready to present the concept to Danny. As Hal and

Stanley said, she should think of it as a big sales presentation, and turn on the charm. Besides, if he turned her down,
what was the harm? They could come up with another idea.
Or, if he bit and agreed to be part of the deal, they could take
his money and get out of town. Alice was ready.

# November 20, 1957 – DANNY

D anny ran out of Alice's apartment to get to his car. He couldn't believe what Alice had just told him, and he didn't have much time to get the cash he needed to buy into the deal. He had a great feeling about this one. And, much as he hated those two wimps Alice hung out with at Underwood, he had to admit they were protecting her and including her even though she had no idea what the investment meant. Danny knew how these companies were bought and sold. This is how you made real money, not by working day by day, but by being part of a big deal. And Danny was sorely in need of a big deal to pay off some gambling debts he had and to maintain the new house and lifestyle he set up in New Jersey. He had to shake his head about that little item. He was paying an unbelievable amount for Dee to live the high life in New Jersey, and he was hocked up to his eyeballs to keep it going. It grated on him that he didn't even like her. This felt like Nora all over again. Dee was just another pain in the ass woman holding him down. And just like Nora, she was dumb. Danny couldn't stand dumb people. He had taken care of Nora and got her out of his life, so it wasn't impossible to think he could take care of Dee when the time came.

But Alice..... she was another story. He loved her looks, her success and her intellect. He had finally found an interesting woman. And to prove to himself that she was worth it, he was about to make a bundle on a sure-fire deal she described. It was almost too good to be true. When the deal closed he could get out from under the debts he amassed in the last year and figure out a way to get rid of Dee and dump Evelyn.

Dumping Evelyn was an interesting idea considering that she was the person he was going to see right now. It had been ten days since he had called her but he was pretty sure she would still want to be with him. He also knew Evelyn and her husband had some cash stashed away. Evelyn had complained that her husband was always telling her not to buy new clothes or cosmetics because they needed to keep saving for the future. If Danny could convince Evelyn to lend about $4,000 to him he could come up with the amount Alice said she needed.

As Alice described it, Hal, Stanley and Alice were approached in strict confidence by the CEO of Underwood about the sale of the company. Underwood was in talks to be sold to Olivetti Corporation and Olivetti wanted to be sure the top salesmen wouldn't leave immediately after the sale closed. Olivetti insisted that Underwood get contracts with noncompete clauses from Hal, Stanley and Alice prior to the sale closing. Alice told Danny that Hal and Stanley had demanded they be sold a part of the company prior to its being sold to Olivetti in exchange for the contracts being signed. The CEO was angry but agreed that they could each buy $5,000 of company stock at the value of the company before it engaged in discussions with Olivetti. When the sale of the company closed that $5,000 would be worth as much as $20,000. Alice didn't have the money because she had just used her savings to buy her new car. She was frantic because Hal and Stanly were very sure they could make three to four times their money when the sale to Olivetti closed. Alice wasn't sure how all of this worked, except that only she could own the shares and only if she signed the new contract. The problem was that she didn't have the money to buy the stock. She had four days to come up with the cash.

Danny told Alice he could front her the money, but she would have to share the profits with him. Alice agreed immediately because without Danny's money she had nothing and with it she would at least have half of the upside. Now Danny was on a mission to find $5,000. He thought he could scrape together about $1,000 from some of his accounts, but it wasn't nearly enough. He was hoping he could convince Evelyn to lend him $4,000. He would have to tell Alice she wasn't going to get half of the upside because he would have to give Evelyn a return for the loan, but that was a small issue he could deal with later. Right now he had to look good, be nice and romance Evelyn so she would agree to give him the money. He thought through how he would present it to her and decided he would call it an investment he already owned which was making great money and would Evelyn like to get into it. He thought that would ease her mind about giving him the money. He hoped she bought the idea.

Three hours later Danny was in bed with Evelyn having just fucked her. She was cuddled up to him and he started talking to her about why he hadn't been around as much. He explained that his new jobs were going very well and kept him busy most of the time. But what was really exciting in his life was a new investment he had that was throwing off great profits. He said the cash was just pouring in. She seemed interested. He knew she liked money and if she had more money she wanted to do more things like shopping for nice clothes and going out to dinner. He looked at her and asked if she was interested in getting involved. He thought he could help her get into the action. Evelyn said she would love to but didn't think her husband would let her. Danny suggested she just get the money and then replace what she took from their account as soon as the cash started coming in. She thought about that and asked how much she would need. He said he thought $4,000 would be good. She asked how quickly she could get the $4,000 back. Danny said he thought it would be a matter of a couple of weeks. She snuggled closer to him and said she would do it.

Danny smiled.

# November 22, 1957 – ALICE

A lice hugged Danny and told him he was wonderful. He twirled her around in the small space in her little apartment and said he adored her. She laughed. The $5,000 cashier's check was on the table for her to deposit into her checking account the next morning. Then she told him she planned to go into the office, buy her shares of the company and sign her noncompete contract. Everything was working out just fine. There was one small problem. Alice couldn't be with Danny tonight. Hal and Stanley had hired a lawyer to review the noncompete contract and they had to meet that night to go over it so they could all sign in the morning. Alice told Danny she was sorry but they would celebrate when the deal for Olivetti closed. Alice was sure it would be reported in all the papers.

Danny nuzzled her neck. He wanted her so much, but he had to agree that Hal and Stanley had surprised him in the way they handled this transaction. He was not going to get in the way of any issues to get those shares purchased and the contracts signed the next day. He had even heard a rumor about the sale of Underwood Company when he was at Penn Manufacturing the day before. He was feeling very good about all of this.

Alice sat down on the sofa and patted the seat next to her for Danny to join her.

"I'm headed to Pennsylvania tomorrow night and I'll be gone for about 5 days. I got a call from my mom yesterday and my dad is not doing well. I think this maybe it. He hasn't been well for about a year and he's just wilting away. If he passes while I'm there I'll stay for the funeral, so I might not be back here for a week or more. Just so you know."

Danny took her hand. He was being very solicitous, which was not usual, but Alice figured he was so taken with the prospect of the deal going through that he wasn't going to be a bastard no matter what she said.

"I get it, baby. Of course you want to be with your mom. I only wish I wasn't so busy at work so I could be with you."

Alice worked very hard to keep smiling and not slap his face. He was such a pig and she couldn't wait to get away from him.

"Ok. I have to leave to see the lawyer. I'll show you out."

Danny took her in his arms and kissed her hard. She responded to keep up the charade, but she relaxed only when he let her go.

"I'll be in touch, baby." He stroked her cheek and walked out the door.

She went to the window and watched him get into his car and drive away. She picked up the phone and called Hal and Stanley who were waiting together at Hal's apartment to hear from her.

"He just left and I have the check. Time to go into action boys." She could hear them laughing on the other end of the line.

"How is the packing going?" Hal asked. "Remember, not

more than 2 suitcases each. It will be hard to muscle more of them on and off the train."

"I'm in good shape. I gave most of my furniture to other people in the building. They are picking it up early tomorrow morning. I will be at the bank by 10 am and I'll deposit the check in the bank account we set up. I should be at the office by 11. How long do you think it will take to meet with our supervisor and clean out our desks?"

Stanley answered. "Not that long. I think we should be done before noon and at the train station by 12:30. There's a train to Chicago leaving at 12:58, hopefully we'll be on it. If we miss it there's one going to St. Louis at 1:45. That's our backup. As long as we can get out of town before tomorrow night we'll be fine. I think the gossip is that the deal with Olivetti will close by the end of the week which means between that announcement and your father's illness, we shouldn't have a problem for the first 5 days. By then we'll be in California."

Alice pictured their new life in the California sun.

Hal suddenly piped up. "Alice we're sorry you had to sell your car. It was easier for us because ours were old jalopies. We can all look forward to buying shiny new convertibles when we get jobs in San Francisco. "

Alice smiled and said good night. Tomorrow was going to be some day.

# November 29, 1957 – DANNY

D anny was beside himself. He made it to the door of the Underwood Company just as he began to retch. His face was hot and his eyes were swimming. He leaned over the rail of the steps and vomited. It had been one week since he was with Alice in her apartment. He tried to call her a few times later that week, but she didn't answer. On Saturday the Hartford Courant newspaper announced the Underwood Company had been sold to Olivetti for a handsome price. He was ecstatic. He wanted to celebrate with Alice on their good fortune, and he wanted to fuck her. He thought this was the end of his troubles and the beginning of a great time with Alice. He was on top of the world.

On Saturday afternoon he got out of the house and away from Dee so he could call Alice's apartment again. He figured that even if her dad had died while she was in Pennsylvania, she should be back from the funeral by Saturday. But when he made the call the telephone number was no longer in service. This made no sense, because Alice told him she would be back and they would celebrate together. He was totally confused.

On Sunday his dumb in-laws were visiting, which meant he couldn't get away. But, first thing on Monday he planned to head for Hartford and see what was going on. He regretted that he never got the name of the town in Pennsylvania where Alice's parents lived. He could have called there and tried to talk with her. He could have asked her if she planned to sell her shares on Monday so they could get the cash. But, he had no idea where in Pennsylvania they lived, other than the "western" part. So, he had to wait. It was torture to put up with Dee's family and make small talk for the entire day on Sunday. He was short and abrupt with everyone, yelling at this niece and nephews and snapping at his wife. He was in such a bad mood that his relatives left early. Fine with him. He could sit and watch the time go by all by himself. The sooner he got to Monday the happier he would be.

On Monday he left work early and headed for Hartford. He got to Alice's apartment just as she should be coming home. He sat outside in the car for about 30 minutes, then decided to go in and see if he could find any neighbors who knew when she returned from her trip. He went into the building and up the stairs to her floor and knocked on her door. There was no answer. Ok, he thought, she could still be in Pennsylvania, she could be working late or out with her dumb salesmen pals, Hal and Stanley, or she could be shopping. He stood in the hall trying to think of the best thing to do next. Her neighbor came up the stairs and said, "Hi."

Danny quickly responded, "Hello there. I'm trying to locate Alice Keene who lives here. Have you seen her since she went to visit her parents in Pennsylvania last Wednesday?"

"Gosh, no. I haven't seen her at all. The only thing I know is she was offering some of her furniture to people in the building but told everyone they had to pick it up by last Wednesday morning. I got her sofa, which looks really nice in my apartment. On Thursday the building superintendent put a note in my mailbox, in fact, in every mailbox, that her apartment was now for rent. I thought she had moved permanently. I didn't think she was coming back. And, to tell you the truth, I don't think the building super thought she was coming back because I know he showed the apartment to another couple over the weekend. Are you sure she said she would be here this week?"

Danny stared at the neighbor with his mouth hanging open. He couldn't believe what he had just heard. His head was racing. Maybe Alice decided to go to a bigger or better apartment, or maybe she was moving in with a roommate. He hadn't called her in a few days so maybe she hadn't had a chance to tell him what she was doing. He wasn't that surprised. She wasn't like a typical woman. She bought her own car, she had a substantial job, she took care of himself. Danny tried to smile and look reassured, but the neighbor was looking at him strangely.

"Are you all right?", he asked. "You look a little shell shocked."

Danny shook his head and folded his arms across his chest. He could feel his heart pounding through his suit jacket.

"No, no problem. I guess I got the message confused. She must have meant I was supposed to go to her new address to meet her, not here. I've been traveling this week and didn't realize she had already relocated. I'll just follow up with her in the new place. Thanks for the info."

He retreated down the stairs as quickly as possible. He had to get to Underwood and find out where she was. He wasn't sure how he could get them to give him her address, but they must know where she is living now, or maybe he could ask about Hal and Stanley. He wished he knew their last names, but the receptionist would know who he was talking about. How many gorgeous redheaded female salesmen did Underwood have working there, and how many of them were best friends with two other successful salesmen? He was sure he could get the info as soon as the company opened the next day. He just had to get through the night.

And here he was, standing outside the Underwood building, retching, trying to understand what he had just heard. The receptionist knew exactly who he was talking about when Danny asked about Alice and her two friends. Unfortunately, she couldn't help him with any addresses or information. Alice, Stanley and Hal had all come into the office late Wednesday morning last week and resigned. The sales manager was in a tailspin and the execs were all running around trying to cover up that they quit so that the sale of the company was not affected by the three top salesmen leaving at the same time.

The receptionist went on to say that it didn't seem to matter much because the sale went through as planned and rumor was that Olivetti was letting the entire sales group go because they had plenty of sales people to cover the territory the Underwood sales group called on. So, she said it was a big tempest in a teapot. Hal, Alice and Stanley left before they were about to be laid off. Some people were even saying they were smart because they had a head start on finding another job somewhere else. But, it seemed, no one knew where else they could find work. It wasn't like Hartford was full of typewriter companies.

Danny straightened up and tried to wipe his lips with his

handkerchief. He had a disgusting taste in his mouth. He couldn't believe that he could be taken like this. Alice had his money and he had no way of knowing where she was. He could look for her, but he also had to work, because now he truly was broke. He owed Evelyn some return on her loan soon since he convinced her the money from the investment came in quickly. He knew she would be very anxious if she didn't get some cash from him by next month. His mind raced. There were so many people he hated at this moment and so many people he wanted to hurt. He wondered if Alice had put together the set up herself or was it all laid out with Hal and Stanley. Somehow, he thought it had to be the three of them. He knew Alice was smart, but this con job was perfect. He had no one to complain to about the cash he gave Alice because he wasn't supposed to know about the share purchase. He wasn't even sure there ever was a share purchase. If the receptionist was right, Olivetti didn't need sales people who worked at Underwood. He couldn't press charges that they had swindled him because if word got out Evelyn would know the loan was not for an investment he already had and worse, was now gone. Evelyn would panic and say he had swindled her. He was gasping for breath as he realized he had been totally fucked by Alice, Hal and Stanley. He had no idea where he could come up with $4,000 to pay Evelyn and he was now in worse shape on his own IOUs because he had used the last of his money to make up the $1,000 Alice needed to buy $5,00 worth of shares. Which, he now had to admit were only "pretend" shares.

"Those fucking bastards. They stole my money, they stole my loan from Evelyn, and they took off without a trace." He wanted to kill all three of them. He wanted to kill Evelyn too. He felt like a fool, a turd and a complete asshole and stooge. Danny Russo never felt like a stooge. He was enraged.

Even when Nora had presented him with her announcement of the baby and his parents had demanded he marry her, he felt he still had options. But this situation was fucking serious and he had to figure out a way to get out of it. Danny Russo couldn't go down for a measly $5,000. He would get it fixed. He had no idea how, but he knew he would get it fixed. Then he would find those fuckers and tear them a new one. He was now on a vendetta, and there was no stopping him.

# March 31, 1958 – DANNY

It was three weeks since Danny met Evelyn on Valley Falls Road in Vernon, Connecticut. He had been very careful during the past three weeks to spend most of his time at his consulting jobs in New Jersey. He wanted to stay away from Connecticut as much as possible. He knew the police would be extra careful in this investigation. There no easy answer to why Evelyn had been shot. This wasn't like when Danny got rid of Nora by using her well-known carelessness with the gas stove while he was supposedly with his brothers at dinner. And this wasn't as tidy as his disposal of Monica's body, which never was found and was probably already decomposed beyond recognition. Evelyn's death would lead to lots of clues and questions. Evelyn was married, had a steady job and had identification on her when she was found. Danny prayed that she hadn't told anyone she was meeting Danny that day. But the more he thought about it he was almost positive she hadn't. She was usually more worried about people knowing they had a relationship than he was. He could be sure she wanted to keep any meeting they had secret. Certainly, she wouldn't have told her husband she was meeting Danny, and it was hard to believe she told anyone at Penn Manufacturing. She was already upset that a few of the girls at Penn made bitchy comments about her "closeness" to Danny. The idea she would tell them anything about Danny or the money he owned her seemed ridiculous.

Danny figured this time he was going to have to talk to the police about Evelyn and their relationship. Up to now it had been easy for him to eliminate Nora and Monica, he could almost call it easy murder, but he didn't think Evelyn would be as easy as the others. He hoped his luck held and no one could pin him to the murder. Danny believed the police would interview him to find out what he knew about Evelyn and ask him where he was the day she died. He went over his story constantly in his head. He wanted to have it as airtight as possible before the police arrived. He followed the story in the papers as it was reported. Initially the police had no idea why Evelyn was on that deserted road or who would have killed her. They were begging the public for help. The reports said the police were examining Evelyn and her husband's Christmas Card list to see who they knew. Danny was sure she had never sent him a Christmas Card. He could breathe easy on that one. He was not happy the police discovered Evelyn recently withdrew $4000 from her bank account. Neither her husband or family knew what she did with the money. Danny thought it was a good thing they had never signed a note or written about the loan.

On the positive side, with Evelyn out of the picture, Danny's money woes were greatly reduced. He was still out the $1,000 he put towards the stock Alice supposedly bought, but at least it wasn't $5,000 anymore. He was relieved he was rid of Evelyn's constant calls and whining because he hadn't paid her back. Alice, there was a name that made Danny see red. He could not get over the way Alice played him and how neatly she disappeared. He checked all around the Hartford area for people hiring salesmen hoping to find some trace of her. He looked into all the spots he knew she used for shopping, getting her hair done and grabbing a bite to eat, but no one had seen Alice in months. He went to the Underwood Company, now known as Olivetti, twice to see if someone could tell him where Alice's parents lived in Pennsylvania, but no one there knew anything about her home town. So much had changed at Underwood since it became part of Olivetti that on his last visit not many people knew who Alice Keene was.

Danny was feeling like the trail for Alice had gone cold. He checked in at the police station and she no longer had a car registered in her name, she no longer had a business sales job anywhere in the Hartford area and she no longer had an apartment. She left no forwarding address. He was so mad when he thought about Alice he could almost taste his anger. But, he would have to put that to the side for a bit. Now he needed to concentrate on what he would say when the police showed up to talk about Evelyn. What he knew he wouldn't say is that he had killed her.

# April 10, 1958 – GEORGE

George Vitas was not happy he had to drive to Scranton again, but his aunt's funeral couldn't be avoided. The whole family had just been in Scranton for Easter with his in-laws. They drove home Easter night. The next day his aunt died so he was taking the whole family back to Scranton for the funeral. His sister in law, Dee, was visiting them from New Jersey so she was coming along. Her husband, Danny, was planning to drive to Scranton from New Jersey for the funeral. Danny would take Dee home from Scranton. Dee did not seem very happy about going back to New Jersey. George understood why. When she lived in Hartford, Dee had a job she loved at Underwood Company and lots of friends. She also had George, Mary and their four children to visit with whenever she pleased. About two years ago Danny abruptly left Penn Manufacturing and decided to move to New Jersey for a new job. He and Dee bought a lovely home in Montclair and Danny picked up two consulting jobs that apparently paid good money. The jobs were as different as could be. One was with Harley Davidson, the motorcycle manufacturer, and one was with a candy maker, Cutter and Sons. Apparently both companies wanted Danny to help with their manufacturing issues.

The problem for Dee was that the house in New Jersey was stuck in the middle of a very suburban neighborhood with large lots and Dee didn't drive. Unlike Hartford, there was no public bus system she could rely upon in the Montclair area. She was completely dependent on other people to take her shopping, to church or anywhere else. Danny often traveled for work so Dee was left home alone and stranded at the house. George thought it depressed her. She was a great gardener and took care of the yard and house while Danny was at work or away, but there was not much else going on in their Montclair neighborhood. George could only think how dreary the isolation must be for Dee.

On the other hand, Dee had put up with worse than isolation since she'd married Danny. The guy was so hard to figure out. George had spent years talking to Mary about why Dee stayed with Danny. In the past decade they all witnessed Danny's horrible bouts of anger and his erratic behavior. George was outraged and threatened Danny after a harrowing "Joy ride" Danny subjected Mary and the kids to. George told Danny that if he ever scared anyone in the family like that again George would "Kill him." Danny apologized and calmed down after that exchange, but George wasn't so sorry when Danny moved to New Jersey and was further away from their daily lives.

George knew other people had issues with Danny. There was more than one time that Mary wanted to "kill" Danny. The worst case being when he "kidnapped" Joey for a cowboy picture on a horse Danny saw in the neighborhood. Mary panicked and called the police, but Danny didn't see anything wrong in taking Joey for a few hours. Especially since the pictures of the three-year old in chaps, boots and a cowboy hat sitting on the horse were so adorable. George shook his head over how mad Mary was at that escapade.

The strange part of Danny was that he was also one of the most helpful, caring and involved men George had ever met. Since Dee brought him home about ten years ago Danny had become the children's favorite uncle. He was always treating them to ice cream and games. He took the kids on motorcycle rides when they visited New Jersey. He spent time with the older kids, Dorothy and Andy, at the local driving range practicing hitting golf balls. He was funny and loving, often hugging multiple children at one time. Danny was a big guy and the kids loved to crawl around on him. He would lay on the floor of their living room with a pillow under his head watching a baseball game and the kids would snuggle up to him and lay on his stomach. Danny never seemed to mind. He came and went around their house as though it was his own. George wondered if Danny loved being around the children because he and Dee did not have any kids.

Danny showered the family with presents. He bought an accordian for Andy, George's older son, and arranged for him to take lessons. He showed up at the house with bags full of great food from the Italian deli in Hartford. They all loved the salami, cheese, peppers and olives. Danny knew that Mary wanted a cabinet in the kitchen, so he arrived one Saturday morning with wood, and tools and built her a beautiful cabinet with shelves and drawers. Mary was ecstatic. Danny took the kids to the amusement park and told them they could get on any rides they wanted. They had the time of their lives. There was no doubt, Danny was a very complicated character and you were never sure which Danny would show up.

But George thought Danny had been acting differently recently. Two Saturdays ago George and Danny went to the race track together. This was nothing unusual because they often went to the track together to play the ponies. But during the drive to the track and when they were placing their bets Danny kept glancing around and saying he felt like someone was following him. He seemed nervous and distracted. George tried to tell him that no one was following them, but Danny couldn't relax. Then two days ago Danny took Andy to the grocery store to pick up some things for dinner and Danny kept asking Andy if he thought someone was following them. Andy mentioned it to George after Danny left for the night. George wondered why Danny was worried he was being followed. But like everything with Danny, there was no use speculating what it meant because anything could be happening.

The one thing George was sure of was that Dee would never divorce Danny. It seemed no matter what he did or how long he disappeared without explanation, Dee was going to stay his wife. George wondered if it was the money and nice life style she was clinging to, but Mary was convinced it was their Catholic upbringing. There was no way Dee was going to defy the church and lose her rights to the sacraments by divorcing Danny. He was her husband for better or worse.

Now George was driving to Scranton for a family funeral. Mary, Dee and the kids were all sitting quietly in the car. The trip seemed long since they had done it the week before. Six hours from when they started they parked in front of Mary's parent's home in Scranton and everyone piled out. It took just a few minutes to move the bags inside and get settled.

George had always liked his in-laws and the feeling was mutual. He couldn't say they had the same feelings about Danny. It helped that George was Lithuanian and spoke

Lithuanian so his mother and father in-law could talk to him freely. Danny, as an Italian, did not know a word of Lithuanian, so his interaction with Dee's parents was limited. But beyond that limitation, George thought his in-laws didn't trust Danny. They had trouble understanding his obviously free spending habits like his big Cadillacs and his constant traveling and being away from home. They thought he neglected Dee, and even though they were careful not to outwardly show their dislike, George saw it plainly. Danny was no different around Dee's mom and dad than he was around anyone else. He was often angry and hot tempered but he also pitched in to make their lives better. The first time he visited their Scranton house he saw they did not have an indoor toilet or bathroom. True to Danny's nature, he immediately went to a plumbing supply house and bought all the piping, fixtures and finishes needed to install a bathroom on a porch outside their kitchen. He created a door from the house to the bathroom with a small vestibule for a linen closet. It took him over three weeks to finish and George helped him with the heavier work over a weekend he spent in Scranton, but it was Danny who was the driving force behind the new bathroom. In the end, the in-laws, who were getting older, no longer had to go to the outhouse or empty chamber pots. George understood his in-laws warm/cold attitude to Danny. It was the same as his.

Mary and the kids were sitting around the large table in the dining room having a cup of tea and some muffins when the doorbell rang. The only person they were expecting was Danny who should be arriving by dinner time. He might have left earlier than he planned, but he wouldn't be ringing the doorbell to come in. They were all wondering who could be visiting. Dorothy went to answer the door and came back to the dining room where they were all sitting with Grandpa and Grandma.

"Dad, I don't know what's going on, but there are three policemen on the porch. They are asking for Aunt Dee."

George looked at Dorothy and then at Mary. This was very strange. He called up to Dee who was upstairs in the guest bedroom. He went out to the porch to see what was going on.

"Hello officers, can I help you?"

The oldest man of the three responded. "We're here to speak with Domicella, known as Dee, Russo. Is she available?"

Danny looked at each of the men and replied, "Yes, I just called her, she'll be down in a second."

Dee came through the door. She saw the three policemen and looked a George with a startled expression. She clearly didn't know what was going on.

"Hi. I'm Dee Russo. Can I help you?"

Again, the oldest spoke. "Mam. We're here to inform you that your husband, Durando Russo, has been arrested on his way here. He won't be joining you this weekend."

Dee was speechless. George stepped in. "Arrested? Danny? What is the charge?"

The same officer looked directly at Dee, "Mr. Russo has been arrested for the murder of Evelyn Smith in Vernon, Connecticut."

Now it was George's turn to be speechless. He couldn't believe he had heard correctly. The porch started to swim before his eyes. Suddenly the officers were lunging towards them. Dee had crumpled to the floor of the porch in a dead faint. The officers were holding her arms and sides so she wouldn't hit her head. George pulled himself together and called for Mary. He bent over Dee as she began to come around. He yelled,

"Get some water, quick."

From the corner of his eye he saw Mary turn on her heal and go back to the kitchen for water. George knew he should take care of Dee, but he wanted to talk to the officers. He had no idea how to handle this situation. By the time Mary arrived with the water the officers had propped Dee against one of the porch chairs and she was sitting up. Her eyes were like dark pools. She looked like she had just seen a death, and maybe she had. Mary brought the water to Dee and George told her to help Dee into the house. He had to speak with the officers.

The two policemen who hadn't spoken helped Dee get to her feet and slowly walked her into the living room of the house. They helped her into one of the chairs and came back to the porch. Dee had started to weep quietly. Mary had no idea what was going on, but she held Dee's hand and rubbed her back hoping whatever had caused this was bearable. Her first thought was that Danny had died. Maybe he was driving like a lunatic again and had missed a curve at a high speed. Whatever it was, it wasn't good.

George spent about 10 minutes talking with the officers. They informed him that Dee would be required to give a statement to the police in Connecticut. They asked George how long he planned to be in Scranton and would he bring Dee back to Connecticut when he returned. George wasn't sure what they would do but he couldn't imagine Dee being alone in New Jersey. He said he thought she would return with him and his family as soon as the funeral they were attending was over. The older officer gave George his card and told him to call him with their final plans as soon as they were confirmed. George said he would and took the card. The officers left.

George walked into the living room of the house and stood in front of Dee.

"Dee, I am so sorry. I think you should think about coming back to Hartford with us until we've got this sorted out."

He thought about that term, "sorted out". How exactly did you sort out that your brother in-law had committed a murder? And, did any of them believe that Danny could kill someone? Sadly, there were moments when George believed Danny could kill someone. He didn't want to say it to Dee, but the last ten years the family had been walking on eggs around Danny's behavior. Maybe there was a really bad side to Danny that was worse than they had ever seen. Maybe Danny was capable of horrible deeds that went way beyond anything Danny had done to them in his worst moments. Maybe Danny was much worse than they imagined. Or, maybe it was a complete mistake and Danny was innocent. It bothered George that his first thoughts were that it could be true. He couldn't envision a good outcome from this.

Mary looked from one to the other, "What on earth is going on?"

Dee looked at her and continued to cry. George looked around to his children and in-laws standing nearby. They all looked scared and confused.

"Children, please go into the other room. I need to speak with your mother and grandparents."

The children backed away quietly. They sensed something was very wrong. Dorothy took Audrey's hand and led her out of the room. Andy and Joey followed. George closed the door after they left and turned to Mary.

"Danny won't be coming here tonight. He's been arrested in Connecticut."

Mary seemed confused.

"In Connecticut? What was he doing there? I thought he was in New Jersey?"

George shook his head.

"I have no idea. That's what the police said." He hesitated and then almost in a whisper he followed with, "the charge is murder."

At the sound of the word "murder" Dee began to wail. Mary's mouth dropped open and she shook her head back and forth.

"No, no it can't be true. How could anyone say he murdered someone? Danny could be difficult, but he wouldn't murder someone, he would be too smart to do that. For God's sake, he's an auxiliary policeman, he knows he would be caught. They must have made a mistake. He needs a lawyer. I am sure this will all get cleared up."

George decided not to voice his doubts. Why should he be the one to accuse Danny when he had no idea of the circumstances of this murder. He turned to his in-laws and patiently, in Lithuanian, told them what the officers said. They were shocked, and immediately said it couldn't be true. George didn't dissuade them of the thought. He was trying to figure out how to handle this with the family.

He asked Mary to put Dee to bed and to stay with her in her room. That way the children could think Dee was not feeling well. He and Mary's mother would feed the kids dinner and put them to bed. He would tell the kids that the police-men came to the house to tell Dee Uncle Danny was not going to be driving to Scranton tonight because he had car trouble. George would figure out what to do next when they went back to Hartford. They would leave right after the funeral on Saturday. George didn't tell Dee that the police wanted a statement from her when she returned to Connecticut. That could wait until they had all had some time to calm down and figure out what this meant.

Mary did as George asked and helped Dee to her bed-room. George and grandma got the kids fed and settled in the two big beds in the guest room on the third floor. George came back to the living room and talked softly with his in-laws about what happened. He knew the murdered person was a woman but he had never heard the name Evelyn Smith be-fore. Whoever this Evelyn was, Danny had a connection to her and George wondered what that could mean.

Mary came downstairs and joined them. They were speaking in Lithuanian so if any children came downstairs and heard them they wouldn't know what they were discuss-ing. After about two hours, George needed to get some sleep. The day had started with his being annoyed he had to drive to Scranton. Now that inconvenience seemed silly compared to their entire family being disrupted by a murder charge. His stomach was churning. How could this have happened? He looked at his good, hard working in-laws as they struggled to understand what the police said Danny did. Because they didn't speak English they were going to have to be helped through this by him and Mary. He looked at Mary, the mother of his four children, but also the sister of Dee. Murder was so far away from Mary's mindset and life experiences it was probably impossible for her to fathom it even happening, much less happened to someone in the family. George was wondering how they would all get through this. No matter what, George knew that he and Mary had to take care of Dee. She had no one else.

The next morning George and Mary were talking about going to their aunt's wake later that afternoon. They wouldn't stay long and would tell everyone that Dee wasn't feeling well so she couldn't come. The funeral was the next day so they planned to be ready to leave right after the service. Mary was wondering if it would be strange for them to skip the luncheon reception after the burial so they could get on the road. She wasn't sure if anyone would notice them not being there. While they were talking Dorothy came into the room and said grandma asked her and Andy to walk to the store which was about four blocks away to get some milk. Mary said that would be fine and gave them some extra money to buy some treats for the children. Audrey especially liked penny candies which they sold at the counter of the local grocery. George asked the kids to pick up a few of the newspapers at the store. He wasn't sure the murder story would be in the papers yet, but he wanted to be sure he knew what was being said if they did report on the story. Dorothy and Andy left for the store and Mary said she was going to go see if Dee was up and dressed. A half an hour later, Dorothy burst through the door of the house holding a stack of newspapers. The headline of the first was "New Jersey Executive Held in Sweetheart Slaying." There was a picture of Danny next to the headline. George's heart sank. This was not going to be contained.

George sat Dorothy and Andy down. At 16 and 14 they were old enough to hear the truth. Andy was very quiet, but Dorothy immediately began to cry.

"What does this mean, Daddy? What do we do?"

"Well, that's a tough question. I don't think we do anything, but continue our lives, you go to school, I go to work. What we have to do is help Aunt Dee because this is going to be very hard for her."

He wrapped his arms around Dorothy and looked at Andy.

"I also hope you will not scare your little brother and sister with any of talk about murders. They wouldn't understand it. Actually, I don't understand it. So, let's all be careful about what we say to each other."

They both nodded their heads in agreement and George took the papers from them. He didn't know how bad the stories were but he had to read them. There was so much they didn't know that any information would be better than no information.

"Andy, please find your mom and ask her to come down to talk to me." Andy went off to find his mom.

Dorothy asked if she could read the stories. George hesitated, but realized that it would be better to have her know what was happening than have her friends at school tell her what they heard. He handed her one of the papers and picked up one to read himself.

They were all deep into the newspapers for the next hour. George spent the following hour translating the stories to his in-laws. It was quite a day of revelations. The biggest surprise was that Danny had already confessed to the murder of Evelyn Smith. Danny claimed he was on his way to Connecticut to give himself up when the State Troopers pulled him over. He said he was innocent because Evelyn had threatened him with a gun. According to Danny's story, Evelyn pointed the gun at him when he got into her car on the deserted road in Vernon and in the ensuing tussle the gun went off. Danny said he shot her but it was in self-defense.

Unfortunately, Danny's version of the story contradicted what the police reported earlier. Evelyn's body was found slumped over the steering wheel of the car. She had her foot on the clutch and she was holding the keys. A cigarette had burned out on her coat. It was unlikely the cigarette would have stayed on the coat or the keys in her hand or her foot on the clutch if the tussle Danny described had happened.

The police reported they had been following Danny for the past four weeks. He became a suspect in the murder when a note Evelyn wrote to him was found in the bottom drawer of her desk at Penn Manufacturing. She had apparently never given or sent the note to Danny. In the note Evelyn demanded that Danny repay the $4,000 she lent him last November for a complex stock purchase deal he was arranging. She told him if he didn't give her the money he had promised she would go to the authorities and turn him in. She also threatened to contact his wife and reveal their affair. This was hard for George to read and harder for him to discuss with Dee. He wanted to ask her if she had any idea Danny had a mistress, but he thought it would be too painful to have that conversation now. George also remembered Danny's worrying about being followed. As it turns out, he was being followed, which meant George and his son were being followed too. This awful nightmare made George's stomach turn. He could not believe that his entire family was now involved in a murder.

Mary was reading the reports along with George. She was in shock. Obviously, there was no need to say to anyone at the wake today that Dee wasn't there because she wasn't feeling well. Dee wasn't there because her life had been destroyed.

The most unreal part of the story was the description of Danny at the scene of the crime with the police officers. As always, Danny was described as being beautifully dressed. What was most appalling was he was also described as happily laughing and discussing what had happened with Evelyn at the scene of the crime as he smoked a cigar with the policemen in their cruiser. George was revolted. How could a man who killed a woman, accident or not, be so cavalier in his attitude about what he did.

The police mentioned that after visiting the scene of the crime Danny broke down and cried, but George thought it was for show. Danny was not only a bad guy but an evil person. George now considered him a murderer. He didn't buy the tussle story. He had heard Danny make up stories to cover what he did so often he knew this was another of Danny's fabrications. And, if he was so eager to give himself up why had he waited for four weeks. George was appalled that over the past four weeks he and his family had spent quite a bit of time with Danny. He couldn't believe he had subjected his family to a murderer. It was frightening.

Somehow George and Mary got through the wake and funeral and packed everyone in the car for the ride back to Hartford. Dee was quiet the whole way home. This was going to be a step by step, day by day situation. They all wanted to talk, but it was hard to know what to say. When someone asked a question they had no answers and Dee would began to cry. None of them knew what was coming or how to deal with what they now knew. The fantasy of Danny being inno-cent and the police making a mistake was gone. Danny was a confessed murderer and in Connecticut he had three options. He could plead innocent and be free if the jury bought his self-defense story, he could go to jail for Manslaughter if he pleaded guilty but convinced the jury there was no premedi-tation, or he could plead innocent and be convicted of first degree murder and put to death.

George kept thinking this couldn't be real. He was a sim-ple person who loved his family and looked forward to raising his kids with his beautiful wife. Having a brother in-law who had a mistress, or maybe several mistresses, and had con-fessed to killing one of his mistresses was totally foreign to him. In his wildest imagination he couldn't have guessed this would ever happen to someone he knew. His goal now was to protect his family. He was only interested in his wife, his children and his sister in-law. He had to keep that thought. If he tried to understand Danny he was lost. It was hard to deal with what this all meant.

The reports on the murder and investigation were head-lines for the next few months. Every new revelation jolted the family. The police tried to dredge the Connecticut River where Danny said he threw the gun parts after leaving the scene of the murder. Their efforts were fruitless. No one ever found the gun. Danny continued to insist he was innocent by way of self-defense. George thought the jury would think otherwise. No one could say Danny didn't have his own gun with him when he went to meet Evelyn. Dee had no idea how many guns Danny had and where he left them. The only gun that was missing was Evelyn's husband's gun. Danny said that because the gun was Evelyn's husband's it proved he hadn't gone to the meeting to kill Evelyn. Danny insisted the gun went off because he fought with Evelyn when she pulled the gun on him. George wondered why Danny shot twice if he was only trying to stop Evelyn from killing him. Wouldn't one shot have been enough? One shot was wild and landed in the lining of the car roof. The other shot hit Evelyn in the neck and head. George thought the jury would have a hard time with two shots being fired and killing Evelyn. Since Danny weighed almost twice what Evelyn did, it was hard to imagine Danny thought Evelyn would wrest the gun back from him.

Then there was the issue of Evelyn's cigarette burning a hole in her coat. It was hard to imagine that in any tussle the cigarette stayed on her coat without falling to the floor. George didn't know how Danny was going to get around the cigarette slowly burning out on her coat. In George's opinion, Danny was in big trouble.

The following week Dee gave her statement to the police in Hartford. George was allowed to sit in as support for Dee. It was a quick interview. George wasn't surprised. What could Dee say? She was home in New Jersey the day before and the day of the murder. Danny didn't come home until late the night of the murder. He seemed normal when he arrived. She warmed up dinner for him, they went to bed, and he went to work the next day. There was nothing surprising or strange in his behavior. Dee said Danny was at the house in New Jersey the entire week. She didn't even know about the murder

because she had not read any newspapers. She knew nothing of Danny's relationship with Evelyn or any other women.
She knew he worked both in Hartford and in New Jersey but
didn't know exactly what he did. She knew he had a secretary when he was at Penn Manufacturing but forgot her name
until she heard he confessed to killing Evelyn. She had no
idea where the $4,000 dollars went. In fact, she had no idea
about any of Danny's money. He gave her cash for groceries and to pay the dry cleaners and she had some extra she
used for her own errands, but other than that, she knew nothing about their finances. George thought she sounded clueless about their life but figured that was how she coped with
how strange and scary Danny was over the years. In George's
opinion, being married to Danny was a terrible waste of Dee's
young life. Hearing her description of Danny's behavior the
night of the murder made George realize how cool a customer
Danny was. It didn't seem to bother him one bit that he had
killed a woman that day. It made George sick.

About a month after the murder Dee asked George to
drive her to see Danny in the Wethersfield prison where he
was being held. George wasn't sure this was a good idea. In
fact, if Mary hadn't stopped him he would have argued long
and hard with Dee to divorce Danny immediately and stop all
connection with him and his crime. It was clear Danny had
been unfaithful and Dee could easily explain her fear of him.
He had terrorized her for years and George thought she could
be divorced based on his abuse. But Mary insisted he not
bring this up. Mary was sure Dee had to come to the divorce
decision herself. She didn't want George to push Dee into
anything she wasn't ready to do.

George and Dee drove in silence to the prison. They were checked into the visitors area and sat waiting for Danny to be brought to them. It was a dull grey room with metal tables and chairs. Two chairs were arranged on one side of each table with visitors looking at the wall. The prisoners sat in the lone chair against the wall looking out to the room. George figured this was the way the officers could monitor the prisoners. They were instructed not to keep their hands on the table. George thought it was strange that they were the only people in the room. Dee baked some cookies for Danny. Before they entered the visiting room the guards opened the cookie tin and turned each cookie over. George thought they were checking to be sure nothing was being smuggled into the prison. They handed the tin back to Dee. Obviously, it had passed their inspection. After about 20 minutes a guard approached them. He spoke directly to Dee.

"I am sorry, but Danny has declined to see you."

Dee looked at the guard and then at George. "I don't understand," she said.

The guard seemed a bit sheepish but continued. "Sorry, but we have no way to force a prisoner to see a visitor. We told Danny you were here with your brother in-law. He asked for a few minutes to think about it and then said he didn't want to see you. I am required to tell you what he said. I am sorry."

Dee stood up suddenly and turned to the door they had entered. She ran out of the room. George moved quickly to catch up with her. She left the cookie tin on the chair she where she was sitting.

# June 14, 1958 – DANNY

D anny looked out the courthouse window and saw the bright sunshine and full trees. Summer had arrived and he was hoping that later today he would walk out and enjoy the beautiful day. That was, after he was acquitted. The day began early when he was ordered to wash, shave and dress for the first day of his trial. His lawyer met him in the small cell he was moved to at the courthouse to review what would happen in the courtroom today. The lawyer wanted Danny to understand that the Judge in the trial was a tough, no nonsense guy. Danny had to be ready for the judge to cut off any extraneous discussions about Danny's life or his actions. The judge would only be interested in the facts leading up to Evelyn Smith's death in Vernon in March. Danny thought he could gain some sympathy with the death of his first wife and child but his lawyer said the judge would not let it be admitted. He also said the judge would not let the Prosecution go on about how Danny treated Dee, his second wife. On balance, Danny thought that might be a fair swap. No one would say he treated Dee well. It would also keep her family off the witness stand, and that was a gift. Of all the people who knew Danny, George, Mary and their son, Andy, had the most damaging information on him. They could site the times he had been out of control and scarred them all, which would highlight his angry outbursts and might show he could be driven to murder if threatened. Andy could testify that he saw Danny with Alice in that coffee shop a few months ago. So far, none of Danny's other girlfriends had surfaced. Danny wanted to keep it that way. Danny was grateful the judge would only be interested in where he and Evelyn intersected, not the other parts of his life.

The lawyer told Danny he had one last chance to change his plea before they swore in the jury. Danny knew that he was on shaky ground on the innocent plea, but he thought he could describe the scene with Evelyn in the car in such detail that the jury would be convinced the gun went off in self-defense. Danny was ready to take the stand to do his part. He knew he could be persuasive and charming and he intended to be both. The idea that he should plead manslaughter which meant rotting in jail for 20 years sounded ridiculous to him. No one put Danny Russo away without a fight. He told his lawyer not to worry. He would convince them all he was innocent. His lawyer was not pleased.

Danny and his lawyer rehearsed Danny's testimony many times. Danny would be the last witness for the Defense. He was prepared to say he really liked Evelyn and was hoping they could work something out about the money. He had no idea she was as frantic as she acted. He would clearly and slowly describe how Evelyn pointed the gun at him when he got in the car and how he pushed her hand back and tried to get the gun away from her. He would continue to say he wasn't sure whose finger was on the trigger when the gun went off. He would describe the first wild shot and how Evelyn continued to pull the gun towards her. He pushed her back against the drivers' door and tried to pull the gun away from her again. She twisted her hand and he followed it with his hand. At that moment the gun was pointed at her and it went off a second time. The bullet hit her in the head. She was dead. He would say how shocked he was and how he pushed away from her and backed out of the car. He then climbed into his car in a fog. He could not believe what had just happened. He didn't remember driving away from the scene of the crime. He was surprised to see the gun on the seat of his car. He would swear he didn't remember having it when he got out of Evelyn's car. He would describe how he stopped when he got to the Charter Oak Bridge and pulled the gun apart and dropped the gun parts into the Connecticut River. He would talk about how badly he was shaking. He would then tell the jury he got back into his car and drove to his home in Montclair, New Jersey. He would insist he never intended to hurt Evelyn, he only went to meet with her so they could figure out a way to get her money back soon. He was thinking of selling some of his hunting trophies and his diamond stick pin to raise the cash. He was worried about her. He would explain that if his investment hadn't gone bad he would have paid her fully as soon as he could. He planned to look right at the jury and say he missed her. He would describe her as a lovely young lady. He would act devastated that it came to this.

They entered the courtroom and Danny wasn't surprised it was so crowded. He knew the press was having a great time with Evelyn's murder. He was getting tired of seeing the description of himself as the "Sweetheart Slayer". The name was used in endless headlines. It didn't help that last month Dee went to court to sue for divorce. Well, he was hardly sorry about that development because it was an easy way to get rid of her. When he walked away free today he would be happy to have Dee off his worry list. But even wimpy Dee produced big headlines when she appeared in court for the divorce. "Sweetheart Slayer Divorced in Superior Court" screamed one of the rags on its front page. Yes, the press was loving the story of Danny taking up with his young secretary, stealing her money and shooting her when she wanted it back. He was surprised so many people thought it was interesting. The press played up his "high" lifestyle as though having a Cadillac, dressing well and living in a house in Montclair, New Jersey was so lavish. He thought it was almost funny that they knew almost nothing about him. It made him think of Nora and Monica. He wondered how incredible the story would seem if the press knew everything about Danny's life in the last twelve years. He had managed to dodge a bullet twice before and he was convinced that he could do it again today.

It also made him think of Alice. The best part of walking free today would be that he would be able to find Alice. That would be Danny's sweetest victory because Alice's scam against him was the moment that made him most livid. How he dealt with Alice would make this circus look tame. He looked around again at the hordes of reporters flashing bulbs in his face. He wondered what they would think if they knew his whole story.

The trial began with lots of dreary talk and tedious lectures. The jury was sworn in and Danny was asked to give his plea. He stood tall in his best grey suit and starched white shirt with a silk tie and said in a strong voice, "Innocent."

A murmur went through the courtroom with that one word.

For the press it was a confirmation: the case was going to go
to the jury after all the evidence was heard. Everyone settled down for a long day of witnesses. The Prosecution presented their witnesses. The people who worked with Evelyn
at Penn Manufacturing testified about seeing Evelyn and
Danny acting like more than a secretary and a boss. There
was lots of speculation about their relationship but no one
had seen them together outside of work. Any relationship
they might have had was only based on gossip. The state
trooper who pulled Danny over in Connecticut and arrested
him said Danny cooperated fully and admitted to being in
Connecticut to give himself up. The detective in charge of
the investigation, a Mr. Taylor, went through the steps in his
investigation and explained how they found the letter Evelyn
wrote to Danny in the bottom drawer of her desk. Danny
hated that the letter existed, but there was nothing he could
do about it. The letter gave the police the information on
the money transfer and made Danny their prime suspect.
They trailed him for about three weeks before they put out a
warrant for his arrest. They found nothing suspicious in his
activities during those three weeks.

The Prosecution had one last witness. It was the youngest of the policemen in the patrol car when they took Danny
to the scene of the crime. Danny couldn't understand why
this young officer named Peter Byrne, was asked to testify.
Everything that happened that day had been described by
Detective Taylor who was in charge of the squad.

Peter Byrne was sworn in and the prosecution asked
him where he was the day Danny was taken to the murder
scene. Officer Byrne explained he was the junior officer in

the group and therefore his job was to sit in the back seat of the patrol car with the accused. He did this. Danny, who knew the other police officers because of his association with the Glastonbury Auxiliary Police program was laughing and talking with the other officers as they stood around the crime scene area on Valley Falls Road. One of the officers brought cigars, so they were all smoking. After a few minutes the officers asked Danny to get into the patrol car to return to the prison. Danny climbed into the car and nodded to the young officer. The officer said he remembered Danny was smiling.

"What's your name?" Danny asked. Peter told him his name. Detective Taylor said they should throw away their cigars before they started back, so the young officer opened the window and Danny threw his cigar out. Danny settled back into the seat. The young officer asked Danny,

"How are you doing?"

Danny shrugged and said. "I'll be OK."

The young officer nodded and said. "That was some meeting you had here on this deserted road."

Danny looked out the window and back at the officer. "Yes, it was," he then hesitated and looked right at Peter Byrne. "But I got her good." Then Danny laughed.

The Prosecutor said, could you repeat that comment please Mr. Byrne? The young officer nodded, "He said, 'I got her good,' and then laughed."

The courtroom exploded in talk and a growling noise. Danny was shocked. He remembered the exchange but couldn't believe the kid had repeated what he said. The cops handling him had all been his buddies. How did this little shit get to repeat his comment? The judge began to bang his gavel to get the court back in order. The Prosecutor asked Peter Byrne to continue,

"I sat next to Danny Russo until we reached the prison. I got out first. Danny climbed out of the car and was escorted into the prison by the officers. That was the last time I saw Mr. Russo until today in the courtroom. "

With that the Prosecution rested its case.

Danny took the stand and did his best to present his version of the meeting with Evelyn. He was as contrite and soulful as he could be, mostly because he now knew his life depended upon it. He thought he did well and the jury bought his line. In true Danny fashion he thought he got away with it.

# Epilogue

Danny Russo was declared guilty of first degree murder and sentenced to death by electrocution. The sentence was carried out on September 14, 1958.

Made in the USA
Columbia, SC
15 January 2020